India Ebook's

ONE SHOT FOR IGNOU MPSE-007

SOCIAL MOVEMENTS & POLITICS IN INDIA

M.A. - Political Science
MPS - 2nd Year

JANMEJOY DAS

INDIA EBOOK PRESS

Contents

1. SOCIAL MOVEMENTS: MEANINGS, SIGNIFICANCE AND COMPONENTS

Introduction
Definition of Social Movements
Social Movements and Political Movements
Extra-Constitutional or non-institutional Path
Importance of Social Movements
Components of Social Movements

1.1: One Shot Concepts

INTRODUCTION

In the early period of political formations social movements shaped the state – its functions, responsibilities as well as accountability and also its political boundary. They also played an important role in distribution of power among various segments in society. In modern times they have played a very important role in challenging the Church and feudal authority, foreign rules and authoritarian regimes. French and Russian revolutions, Indian freedom movement, various peasant movements have profound impact on our life. The fascist movement in Germany, Islamic movement in Middle east, Hindutva movement in India or Tamilian movement in Sri Lanka have not only influenced political system but also value system of the people.

Understanding of social movements is important not only for all those who are dissatisfied with the present social and political order but also to those who are contented with the system to understand fragility of the political institutions and their future. Any socially sensitive person, no matter one is activist or academic, one is sympathetic or critic of the political system cannot ignore social movements of the time. Our understanding of nature of political institutions and their working, nature of Constitution, political decisions and legislation remain incomplete without understanding social movements.

DEFINITION OF SOCIAL MOVEMENTS

In common parlance, media and political circles the term 'social movement' is often used loosely conveying different meanings. Sometimes it is used to show a historical trend like modernisation or urbanisation. The term is also used to indicate a set of activities undertaken by one or many organisations to bring 'change' in society such as education movement launched by the government department of education for starting schools and enrolling students. It is also used for collective action of a segment of society. The phrase social movement is in vogue among political leaders and social activists to camouflage their political activities.

However, the term 'social movement' gained currency in European languages in the early nineteenth century. This was the period of social upheaval. Church and authority the absolute power of the monarchs were challenged. People were demanding democratic rights and asserting for freedom and equality. The political leaders and authors who used the term 'social movement' were concerned with the emancipation of the exploited classes and the creation of a new society by changing property relationships. Their ideological orientation is reflected in their definition. Hence there is no one definition of 'social movement.' Scholars and social activists have different ideological positions on political system and expected social change.

SOCIAL MOVEMENTS & POLITICAL MOVEMENTS   Book Q.5

More often than not, 'social' and 'political' movements are treated more or less the same — except those collective efforts which are mainly and so far confined to personal salvation in relation to supernatural power and do not relate to social structure and within as well as inter-community relationship. But the same movement when it enters in the arena of social relationship affecting public domain it gets character of political movement.

For instance community's collective struggle for sanskritisation is though social movement, it also challenges existing power relationship as community asserts not only higher status but also compete with those who dominate. Backward caste movement is a case in point. Rudolf Heberle (1951) argues that all movements have political implications even if their members do not strive for political power. However, some scholars like Andre Gunder Frank and Marta Fuentes (1987) make a distinction between social and political movements. According to them, the former does not strive for state power. Social movements 'seek more autonomy rather than state power'. There is a difference between social and political power, and the latter is located in the state alone.

Social movement involves any collective struggle aiming at bringing social transformation questioning prevailing hegemony and dominance, property relations, power relations, assertion for identity against the perceived adversaries and resisting dominance; struggle for justice, involves capturing or influencing political authority, though it may not be on the immediate agenda. Therefore, in the present context, the difference between 'social' and 'political' movement is merely semantic.

EXTRA-CONSTITUTIONAL OR NON-INSTITUTIONAL PATH

Book Q.6 **Direct Action**

Social movements follow 'institutional' as well as non-institutional path. The former may be called constitutional and the latter is considered as extra-constitutional or illegal path. Extra–constitutional path is also called '**direct action**' against the state or government.

The action which is legally permitted and 'widely accepted as binding in society or part of society' at a given point of time is institutionalised action. Such actions include petitioning, voting in elections, and fighting legal battles in courts of law. They themselves are not called as social movements as they are part of institutional mechanism and functioning. But when these methods are accompanied by other collective actions and are used as tactics they become a part of the movements.

According to **Rajni Kothari**, 'direct action can be defined as an extra constitutional political technique that takes the form of a group action, is aimed at some political change directed against the government in power' (1960).

A line between legal and illegal or constitutional and extra-constitutional is very thin and ticklish. It is a matter of interpretation of law and constitution. Those who are in authority or support the status quo can interpret a particular action as illegal; but those who strive for social change may interpret the same action as legal. For many, violent means is illegal therefore not permitted. The term 'extra-constitutional' can be a matter of interpretation. Non-institutionalised collective action takes several forms, such as, protest, agitation, strike, satyagraha, gherao, riot, etc.

IMPORTANCE OF SOCIAL MOVEMENTS — Book Q.1

Many political philosophers and leaders conceive the ideal political system and social order. They plead for a necessity and sometimes inevitability of social movements including a revolutionary movement to oppose the 'present' political regime and the system and to establish the system which they consider 'ideal' and perfect capable to resolve the problems of society.

The assumption that the ideal political system is ipso facto capable of resolving all conflict in society is simplistic. Such view is dangerous for democratic social order. There is not, and cannot be an end of history; the final destination and fool proof system. This is not a static concept of political system and society. Each society has its own contradictions.

Social movements provides a possibility for articulation of grievances and problems. They bring pressure on the state, keep check over the authority needed for healthy democracy. Social movement is way of people's/segment's collective politics to express their aspirations and priorities. Without understanding politics of the people we cannot understand complexities and dynamics of political system.

COMPONENTS OF SOCIAL MOVEMENTS — Book Q.4

Social movements have **five main componants**: Objectives, ideology, programmes, leadership, and organisation.

They are interdependent, influencing each other. As discussed above emotional outcry of group of people in the form of crowd is not social movement. Social movement is related to social and political change. So it has an immediate and long term objective. The immediate objective may be to resolve a particular issue or protest against the decision of the authority.

For the long term objective the movement evolves strategy for action. It gives priorities to certain programmes over others, and also focuses on a particular direction, mobilises certain groups. The path of action is closely related to or get evolved with the notion of the desired social change.

It involves a set of ideas, propositions and values that enable to perceive in particular manner social reality. The set of ideas and ideals form ideology. The ideology is not necessarily well-knit, nor always preconceived.

In some cases ideology directs the movement and in other cases ideology gets evolved and directs the movement. Leadership plays important role in articulation of ideology and evolving strategies for action.

Social movement involves mobilisation of people who in course of the process identify with the objective of the movement. They share values and begin to share perception of common understanding of social reality. For their mobilisation and to sustain their participation, the leader(s) evolve different programmes. This also requires some kind of organisation. The organisation may be loose or well formed with centralised or decentralised decision-making system for launching programmes.

1.2: IGNOU Book Exercise – Solved

1) What is the importance of a study of social movements in understanding politics?

Answer by India Ebook: Read the 1 Shot Concept Above.

2) Explain difference between riot and social movement.

Answer by India Ebook: Riots and Social Movements are not same thing. Action of a mob in streets is though a collective behaviour, it cannot be called a social movement. For instance when a mob at the railway station stops a train for misbehaviour of railway staff or prefer to travel without ticket can not be called social movement. Nor riots between two ethnic groups or act of looting food grains from shops or destruction of public property can be called so. These acts by themselves are not social movements. They may be a part – one of the programmes of the social movement.

Strictly speaking, agitation or protests are not social movements. Because, they more often than not, do not aim at bringing social change. They do not conceive that. They are reaction to a particular situation. But at the same time, more often than not, a social movement develops in course of time, and it begins with protest or agitation which may not have conceived the notion of political change. For instance, when students of the engineering college in Gujarat protested against the Mess bill, it was a relatively spontaneous act. But that protest led to the Nav Nirman Andolan of 1974 in Gujarat.

Moreover, a particular collective action may be only an agitation for some scholars, and a movement for others, depending upon the level of analysis and the perspective.

For example, the collective action of a section of society demanding the formation of linguistic states in the 'fifties was viewed as an 'agitation' by some and as a 'movement' by others. Similarly, though riots are not social movements, they are more often than not part of ongoing movements.

3) What are the common elements of different definitions of social movement?

Answer by India Ebook: There are three (3) important elements of the definition of Social Movement. They are

(1) collective action;

(2) social change and

(3) common purpose.

Collective action for bringing 'social change' is an important dimension of definition of social movements. Of course the collective action for maintaining or not disturbing social change as perceived by others is also social movement. Such collective action for status quo may be called counter–movement. Moreover, there is no one meaning of social change. This is evident from the following sample definitions of social movements used in social science literature.

• According to **Herbert Blumer**. "Social movements can be viewed as collective enterprises to establish a new order of life. They have their inception in the condition of unrest, and derive their motive power on one hand from dissatisfaction with the current form of life, and on the other hand, from wishes and hopes for a new scheme or system of living."

• For **Doug McAdam**, social movements are "those organized efforts, on the part of excluded groups, to promote or resist changes in the structure of society that involve recourse to noninstitutional forms of political participation."

• Social movements are, according to **Sidney Tarrow**, "collective challenges, based on common purposes and social solidarities in sustained interaction with elites, opponents and authorities".

4) Which are the main components of social movements?
Answer by India Ebook: Read the 1 Shot Concept Above.

5) What is the difference between 'social' and 'political' movements?
Answer by India Ebook: Read the 1 Shot Concept Above.

6) Explain the term 'direct action'.
Answer by India Ebook: Read the 1 Shot Concept Above.

1.3: IGNOU Past 6 Attempts Question – Solved

Dec 2018: How important are social movements in democratic nations? Elaborate.

June 2019: Explain the meaning and importance of Social Movements.

June 2020: Explain the meaning and importance of social movements.

Answer by India Ebook: The term 'social movement' is often used loosely conveying different meanings. Sometimes it is used to show a historical trend like modernisation or urbanisation. The term is also used to indicate a set of activities undertaken by one or many organisations to bring 'change' in society such as education movement launched by the government department of education for starting schools and enrolling students. It is also used for collective action of a segment of society. The phrase social movement is in vogue among political leaders and social activists to camouflage their political activities.

Many political philosophers and leaders conceive the ideal political system and social order. They plead for a necessity and sometimes inevitability of social movements including a revolutionary movement to oppose the 'present' political regime and the system and to establish the system which they consider 'ideal' and perfect capable to resolve the problems of society.

The assumption that the ideal political system is ipso facto capable of resolving all conflict in society is simplistic. Such view is dangerous for democratic social order. There is not, and cannot be an end of history; the final destination and fool proof system. This is not a static concept of political system and society. Each society has its own contradictions.

Social movements provides a possibility for articulation of grievances and problems. They bring pressure on the state, keep check over the authority needed for healthy democracy. Social movement is way of people's/segment's collective politics to express their aspirations and priorities. Without understanding politics of the people we cannot understand complexities and dynamics of political system.

June 2019: What are the components of social movements? Elaborate.
Dec 2020 (Feb21): What are the components of Social Movements?
Dec 2021: Explain the meaning and components of social movements.
Answer by India Ebook: Same as **Q.4** Above.

NOTES

2. APPROACHES TO STUDY SOCIAL MOVEMENTS: LIBERAL, GANDHIAN AND MARXIAN

Introduction
The Marxist Approach
Structure – Function Approach
Gandhian Approach
Resource Mobilisation Theory
Relative Deprivation Theory

2.1: One Shot Concepts

INTRODUCTION   Book Q.1

Facts do not speak for themselves. They have to be collected, arranged, categorised and interpreted. One collects particular kind of 'facts' and another observer collects different kinds of 'facts' of the same event. Both give different meanings and arrive at different conclusions of the same event. There is no one way of looking social facts and processes.

The same movements can be constructed and interpreted in many different ways, depending upon theoretical perspective from which one looks at the phenomena. **Theoretical perspective or approach** guides the selection of facts, their arrangement, classification and interpretation. One gets better understanding of the process with more systematic and rigorous perspective than casual and unsystematic way of looking the phenomena.

There are **different approaches** to study social movements. But at the same time we should remember that empirical processes are not neat to fit into any one approach. Social and political processes are complex and have their own logic. Moreover, no approach is in pure form. There are variations among the followers of the same theoretical perspective. There are different perspectives among the Marxists and also among the liberals. What is provided here is a broad framework, as guide of a particular approach.

MARXIST APPROACH   Book Q.2

According to the Marxist approach conflict is the central core of social movements. There are different kinds of conflicts in society. Some conflicts are between individuals for personal power, style of functioning, between the communities—social, ethnic, religious, regional etc.— and other conflicts are around material interest and domination of one over the others. The nature of the non-class conflict varies from society to society and can be resolved through negotiations and institutional mechanism. Sometimes though not always such conflict is in a garb of 'class'/economic conflict. That is, economic conflict of different classes belonging to separate communities take the form of ethnic conflict. **Class conflict** is located in economic structure of society, in-built in the production and distribution system. It is around domination and subjugation between the classes. Those who own means of production dominate social and political system. In all forms of class society specific form of production predominates, which influences other forms of social relations.

Those who own and control the means of production take away the surplus from those who produce. They accumulate surplus for their end and expand and perpetuate their control over the society. The former may be feudal lord in feudal system or industrial bourgeois in capitalist system. Antagonistic interests between the propertied and labour classes are inherent in a class-based society that generates contradictions. The former use the coercive as well as persuasive power of the state, and also other institutions, including religion, culture, education, mass media etc, to perpetuate their hegemony in society and to control the exploited classes. The latter resist, protest and occasionally revolt or launch organised and collective action against the dominance of the propertied classes. It is their effort to bring about revolutionary political change by overthrowing the dominant classes in power. In short, class struggle is the central driving force for resistance. Such collective actions take the form of social movements.

STRUCTURE — FUNCTION APPROACH   Book Q. 4

There is a great deal of variation amongst the non-Marxist scholars, in their approach to the analysis of social movements. The ideological positions regarding a need for social and/or political change, and the role of movements therein differ. It is argued by several liberal scholars such as William Kornhauser, Robert Nisbet, Edward Shils and others that mass movements are the product of mass societies which are extremist and anti-democratic. These scholars are in favour of excluding the masses from day-to-day participation in politics, which hampers the efficient functioning of the government.

Some Indian scholars who approved of the agitation for independence from foreign rule, did not favour agitation by people in the post-independence period. They condemned them outright as 'dangerous' and **'dysfunctional'** for 'civilised society'. Though some other liberals do not favour revolutionary change in the political and economic structure, they advocate 'political change' which is confined to change in government and political institutions. A few are for 'revolutionary' change but they differ from Marxist scholars in class analysis.

They lay emphasis on political institutions and culture. In their analysis of the movements, some do not inquire into social and economic causes of conflict and collective struggles. Others differ in their emphasis on the causes responsible for the movements. Some emphasise individual psychological traits, some focus on elite power struggles and their manipulation; and some others emphasise the importance of cultural rather than economic factors.

GANDHIAN APPROACH   Book Q.5

"**Purity of means**" in social struggles and resolving conflict is the central concern of Gandhian ideology. According to Gandhi the means are as important as the ends in resolving conflict. For that he strongly advocated ahinsa i.e. non-violence. Violence he believed, was not only wrong, it was a mistake. It could never really end injustice, because it inflamed the prejudice and fear that fed oppression. For Gandhi, unjust means would never produce a just outcome. "The means may be likened to a seed, the end to a tree," he wrote in 1909, "and there is just the same inviolable connection between the means and the end as there is between the seed and the tree... We reap exactly as we sow."

Gandhians advocate a need for resistance of those who are the victims and suffer against injustice. The method of resistance was satyagraha i.e satya (truth) and agraha (institance, holding firmly). Bondurant (1988) has called this approach the "Gandhian dialectic." Satyagraha was a dialectical process where non-violent action (antithesis) engages existing structures of power (thesis) in a truth-seeking struggle leading to a more just and truthful relationship (synthesis).

In this technique the victims oppose unjust law and also the act of the oppressor/ foreign ruler/landlord/upper caste. They even break the 'unjust' law and in consequence suffer punishment imposed on them by the authority. Such peaceful resistance, Gandhi believed, would open the eyes of oppressors and weaken the hostility behind repression; rather than adversaries being bullied to capitulate, they would be obliged to see what was right, and that would make them change their minds and actions.

RESOURCE MOBILISATION THEORY   Book Q.7

Resource Mobilisation theory is an outcome of rational choice theory. It is based on the assumption that individuals' actions are motivated by goals that express their preferences. They act within the given constrains and available choices. It is not possible for all individuals to get all that they want; they must make choices within the available possibilities at a given point of time. Rational choice theories argue that individuals must make a rational choice regarding what is the best for them in a situation; and accordingly anticipate and calculate the outcome of their actions.

Resource mobilisation theory (RMT)

• Reacts against the older view of social movements (e.g. Communism, Nazism) as an irrational protest of the marginalised and as tending to "extremism" (and so illegitimate and "not really political")

• Sees social movements (e.g. black civil rights, environmentalism) as individually rational attempts to mobilise resources in pursuit of "politics by other means" - hence driven by people with resources, embedded in stable networks (and so legitimate political actors!)

• Tends to reproduce professional organiser's perspective (e.g. Greenpeace, Amnesty): tackling the "free rider" problem to build strong and effective movements (Freeman) through organisation and selective incentives for participation.

The theory emphasises entrepreneurial skill of the leaders of the movements. They mobilise resources — professional, finances, moral support and networking- from within and outside to sustain their struggles. The leaders of the succesful movements have skill to create organisation and mobilise people. In the process common goals are articulated and consensus is created so that all the participants accept the goals.

RELATIVE DEPRIVATION THEORY	Book Q.8

The theory of relative deprivation developed by **American scholars (Gurr 1970)** has also guided some studies on agitation and mass movements.

Relative deprivation is defined as actors' perception of discrepancy between their value expectations and their environment's apparent value capabilities. Value expectations are the goods and conditions of life to which people believe they are justifiably entitled. The referents of value capabilities are to be found largely in the social and physical environment; they are the conditions that determine people's perceived chances of getting or keeping the values they legitimately expect to attain.

Gurr also links three other concepts to relative deprivation, namely dissonance, anomie and conflict. The second of these, anomie is important in its effect to value opportunities. There are three models as to how the differentiation of value expectations and value capabilities has impact on relative deprivation. Decremental deprivation model describes the situation where the expectations are stable but capabilities declines. In aspirational model the capabilities remain the same but the expectations increase. The last model, J-curve or

progressive deprivation model, fits to the situations when expectations and capabilities first increase hand in hand but then capabilities stop to increase or decrease while expectations still go on.

2.2: IGNOU Book Exercise – Solved

1) What is the importance of theoretical framework in understanding social movements?

Answer by India Ebook: Read the 1 Shot Concept Above.

2) What is the significance of "class conflict" in Marxist framework to analyse social movements?

Answer by India Ebook: Read the 1 Shot Concept Above.

3) How 'subaltern studies' approach differs from the mainstream Marxist approach?

Answer by India Ebook: For Marxists, social movements are just not a protest and expression of the grievances. The exploited classes are not interested in reforming this or that institutions though they do fight for incremental rights to strengthen their strength. For instance working class fights for more wages, regulation of work, social security and also participation in management. Through this they build up solidarity among the workers and expand their struggles. Ultimately their attempt is to crack the dominant political system so that in the process the struggles move in the direction of revolutionary changes in the ownership of means of production and over through the dominant state structure.

There is a good deal of debate among Marxist scholars on theoretical and methodological issues. Recently a group of Marxist historians, the **'Subaltern Studies'** group, has begun to study 'history from below'. They criticise the 'traditional' Marxist historians for ignoring the history of the masses, as if the 'subaltern' classes do not make history of their own, depending solely on the advanced classes or the elite for organisation and guidance.

It is argued that the traditional Marxist scholars have undermined cultural factors and viewed a linear development of class consciousness (Guha 1983). On the other hand, the Subaltern Studies historians are strongly criticised by other Marxist scholars for ignoring structural factors and viewing 'consciousness' as independent of structural contradictions. They are accused of being Hegelian 'idealists'.

4) Is social movement dis-functional to the functioning of political system? Why?

Answer by India Ebook: Read the 1 Shot Concept Above.

5) "Purity of means is the central to Gandhian approach" Explain.

Answer by India Ebook: Read the 1 Shot Concept Above.

6) Explain the main features of Gandhian form of Satyagraha.

Answer by India Ebook: Mahatma Gandhi, the leader of India's freedom movement has a far reaching influence on social movements in India during his life time and in the post-independent India. During his life time he led struggles not only against the British rule but also racial discrimination in South Africa, against untouchability and 'discrimination' to women. According to Gandhi the means are as important as the ends in resolving conflict. For that he strongly advocated ahinsa i.e. non-violence.

The potential of satyagraha to change an opponent's position, Gandhi believed, came from the dependence of rulers on the co-operation of those who had the choice to obey or resist. While he continued to argue that satyagraha could reveal the truth to opponents and win them over, he often spoke of it in military terms and planned actions that were intended not so much to convert adversaries but to jeopardise their interests if they did not yield. In this way he made satyagraha 'a realistic alternative' for those more interested in what could produce change than in what conscience could justify.

The method of satyagraha is often called as "passive resistance". But Gandhi made the distinction between the two. In 1920, he argued that they were not synonymous. Passive resistance is generally practice by the weak and non-violence is not their credo. Sometimes it has narrow self-interest which fail to reach out the opponent.

7) Discuss Resource Mobilisation theory in social movement literature.

Answer by India Ebook: Read the 1 Shot Concept Above.

8) Explain the importance of Relative Deprivation theory in the analysis of social movements.

Answer by India Ebook: Read the 1 Shot Concept Above.

2.3: IGNOU Past 6 Attempts Question - Solved

Dec 2018: Compare and contrast Gandhian and Marxist approaches to social movements.

Dec 2020(Feb21): Compare the Gandhian and Marxian frameworks of studying social movements in India.

Answer by India Ebook: Read the 1 Shot Concept Above.

June 2019: How different are the Gandhian and Liberal approaches for studying social movements?

Answer by India Ebook: Read the 1 Shot Concept Above.

June 2020: Discuss the liberal and Marxian approaches to the study of social movements.

Answer by India Ebook: Read the 1 Shot Concept Above.

June 2021: What is liberal approach to the study of social movements? How does it compare and contrast with other approaches?

Answer by India Ebook: Read the 1 Shot Concept Above.

Dec 2021: Explain the Theory of Relative Deprivation.

Answer by India Ebook: Same as **Q.4** Above.

3. CLASSIFICATION OF SOCIAL MOVEMENTS INCLUDING NEW SOCIAL MOVEMENTS

Introduction
Reform, Rebellion and Revolution
New Social Movements
Issue-based Movements
Classification by Social Categories

3.1: One Shot Concepts

INTRODUCTION

Classification is a way of selecting and arranging facts/data. It is a way to give meaning to one's observations. There is no the way of classifying any social phenomenon, process or group of people. Social movements also do not have the only one way of classification. No classification is sacrosanct and universal acceptable by all the scholars and activists. Classification is related to theoretical framework and the question that one wants to understand? Same movement can be classified in several ways depending upon the focus of the study. For instance a collective struggle of people raising issue of pollution can be called environment movement and also human rights movement or middle class movement or reformist movement or new social movement.

REFORM, REBELLION AND REVOLUTION

According to this theoretical perspective social movements are of three types: revolt or rebellion, reform, and revolution.

Revolt or rebellion protests against the political system or regime and may also make attempts to change in the authority – government and/or ruling elite/ rulers. But it does not question nor it aims at changing the political system. In short, the movement is against the regime rather than the system.

- A revolt is a challenge to political authority, aimed at overthrowing the government.
- A rebellion is an attack on existing authority without any intention of seizing state power to change the system.

Reform: The social movement which aims at bringing certain changes in the system and not transforming the system completely is called reformist movement. Such movements question the functioning of political institutions and build pressure on the government to introduce certain changes in their structure and procedures. While doing so they do not question the political system as a whole; nor do they relate a political institution with the larger political structure. In other words they focus on reforming a particular part of an institution or the system. For example, the movement that primarily aims at changing election rules and procedures does not relate elections with the economic structure and power relationship in society.

Revolution: In a **revolution**, a section or sections of society launch an organised struggle to overthrow not only the established government and regime but also the socio-economic structure which sustains it, and replace the structure by an alternative social order. For instance the **Naxalite movement** is not only challenging the particular government but aims at over-throwing the state which is feudal/semi–feudal and desires to establish communist state. Or the dalit movement aims at transforming social order based on caste system and desires to create egalitarian social system. In the same way when women movement challenges patriarchy in society and attempts its abolition then it becomes revolutionary movement.

NEW SOCIAL MOVEMENTS   Book Q.3

The classification based on Marxist theoretical framework focusing on class structure of the participants, with ultimate objectives to overthrough the present state aiming at bringing total change in production relation is considered as 'old' social movement. They are also called classical movements. These movements, it is argued, primarily focus on the state power and on class consciousness of the participants. The examples of the peasant or working class movement against the feudal/semi-feudal economic structure fall in this category.

As against this, some of the recent movements particularly in and after the 1960s in Europe such as peace movement, ecological movement, women's movement etc. are called 'new' social movement. In India the movements around the issue of identity – dalit, adivasi, women, human rights, environment etc. are also labeled as the **'new' social movement**. In one sense they are called 'new' social movements because they have raised the issues related to identity and autonomy which are non-class issues and do not confront with the state. They are the new forms of social movements. However, it is simplistic to say that in the past people did not raise and struggled for identity and autonomy. For instance the **Birsa Munda movement** in Chhota Nagpur during the 1830s was the struggle to resist the intervention of the British state in their life. It was the movement to protect their autonomy.

Following are the characteristics/features of the new social movements: Book Q.4

1) The New Social Movements (NSM) are not directing their collective action to state power. They are concerned with individual and collective morality.

2) The new social movements are not class–based. They are multi-class. In fact, they do not subscribe to the theory that society is divided on class line and the classes are antagonistic. The new social movements are either ethnic or nationalist and plural. Women's movement is an example. Gail Omvedt treats the contemporary farmers' movement as 'new' and non-class movement. It is a movement of small and poor as well as middle and rich farmers. These movements, she argues also have support of agriculture labourers. It also has support of shopkeepers and also of high and low castes.

3) The new social movements are confined to and concern with civil society. According to the proponents of NSM "civil society is getting diminished; its social space is suffering a shrinkage and the 'social' of the civil society is eroded by the controlling ability of the state. The expansion of the state, in the contemporary setting, coincides with the expansion of the market.

4) NSMs are not around economic issues of land, wages or property. They are primarily concerned with self- identity and autonomy of an individual and community against the state, market and social institutions. Therefore, dalit movement for dignity and adivasis movement for their autonomy are treated as NSM.

5) NSMs are not concerned for the benefit of one class or group. They are concerned for the good of every one irrespective of class. Environmental movement in that sense according to some scholars, is NSM as it does not raise the issue of a particular class.

6) For some NSMs are grassroots or micro movements and do not have to capture state power on their agenda. They are democratic in their organisational structure.

ISSUE-BASED MOVEMENTS Book Q.5

Some of those who follow structure-function approach classify social movements on the basis of issues around which people are mobilised. People do get mobilised around number of issues from local and immediate to systemic and long term. They vary from time to time and from society to society. Some times the issue–based classification treat different issue separately. Sometimes issues are conceptualised in theoretical framework such as developmental, livelihood, human Right issues or political, economic, cultural and social issues; or local, regional and national issues. Classification of the issues depends upon scholars' perspective. For instance the movement of the dam affected people can be called as 'rehabilitation' movement of dam-affected people and it can also be called as anti-development movement or human right movement. Similarly, struggles of the forest-dwellers can be classified into: forest movement, civil rights or livelihood movement or movement for common resources.

CLASSIFICATION BY SOCIAL CATEGORIES Book Q.6

Classification is a tool for analysis. It is closely related with theoretical framework. Hence classification of social movements vary from scholar to scholar depending upon his/her analytical framework. Now a days social movements are classified into (1) old or classical and (2) new. The former falls into Marxist framework. It is based on the objectives and class characters of the participants. New social movements are those which are of non-class and around the issues of identity and autonomy. Movements are also classified by issues and/ social class of the participants.

Those who follow Marxist frame work often classify social movements on the basis of classes such as peasant movement or rich peasant movement, working class movement or middle class movement and so on. Those who follow cultural or community framework divide movements on the basis of community such as ethnic movement, western movements, black movement, dalit movement etc. Sometimes social categories are divided by region such urban and rural. Movements may also be classified on economic as well as ethnic categories and also by issues together. Some others classify movements on the basis of the participants, such as peasants, tribals, students, women, dalits, etc. In many cases the participants and issues go together.

3.2: IGNOU Book Exercise – Solved

1) "No classification of social movements is sacrosanct" Explain.

Answer by India Ebook: Classification is a tool for analysis. It is closely related with theoretical framework. Hence classification of social movements vary from scholar to scholar depending upon his/her analytical framework. Now a days social movements are classified into (1) old or classical and (2) new. The former falls into Marxist framework. It is based on the objectives and class characters of the participants. New social movements are those which are of non-class and around the issues of identity and autonomy. Movements are also classified by issues and/ social class of the participants.

Classification is a way of selecting and arranging facts/data. It is a way to give meaning to one's observations. There is no the way of classifying any social phenomenon, process or group of people. Social movements also do not have the only one way of classification. *No classification is sacrosanct and universal* acceptable by all the scholars and activists.

Same movement can be classified in several ways depending upon the focus of the study. For instance a collective struggle of people raising issue of pollution can be called environment movement and also human rights movement or middle class movement or reformist movement or new social movement.

2) Discuss the difference between reform and revolutionary movement.

Answer by India Ebook: **Reform:** The social movement which aims at bringing certain changes in the system and not transforming the system completely is called reformist movement. Such movements question the functioning of political institutions and build pressure on the government to introduce certain changes in their structure and procedures. While doing so they do not question the political system as a whole; nor do they relate a political institution with the larger political structure. In other words they focus on reforming a particular part of an institution or the system. For example, the movement that primarily aims at changing election rules and procedures does not relate elections with the economic structure and power relationship in society.

Revolution: In a **revolution**, a section or sections of society launch an organised struggle to overthrow not only the established government and regime but also the socio-economic structure which sustains it, and replace the structure by an alternative social order. For instance the **Naxalite movement** is not only challenging the particular government but aims at over-throwing the state which is feudal/semi–feudal and desires to establish communist state. Or the dalit movement aims at transforming social order based on caste system and desires to create egalitarian social system. In the same way when women movement challenges patriarchy in society and attempts its abolition then it becomes revolutionary movement.

3) Why 'new' social movements are called 'new'?

Answer by India Ebook: Read the 1 Shot Concept Above.

4) What are the main features of 'new' social movements?

Answer by India Ebook: Read the 1 Shot Concept Above.

5) Give some examples of issue–based movements.

Answer by India Ebook: Read the 1 Shot Concept Above.

6) Give examples of classification based on social classes.

Answer by India Ebook: Read the 1 Shot Concept Above.

3.3: IGNOU Past 6 Attempts Question - Solved

Dec 2018: Write notes in about 200 words on each of the following:
(b) New Social Movements.

Dec 2020(Feb21): What are the new social movements?

June 2021: Describe the New Social Movements (NSMs).

Answer by India Ebook: Same as **Q.3** Above.

June 2019: Critically analyse the characteristics of the new social movements.

Answer by India Ebook: Same as **Q.4** Above.

June 2021: What are the differences between reform and revolutionary movements?

Answer by India Ebook: Same as **Q.2** Above.

Dec 2021: Make a distinction between old and new social movements.

Answer by India Ebook: Read the Concept and di it yourself.

4. DEMOCRATISATION & CHANGING NATURE OF INDIAN SOCIETY

Introduction
Social Reforms and Inequalities During Colonial Period
The Idea of Social Transformation in the Wake of Independence
People's Movements as Reflection of Democracy and Social Change
Backward Classes' and Dalits' Challenge to the Dominance of Upper Castes
State, Democracy and Change
> Caste
> Gender
Liberalisation, Poverty and Social Change
Human Development Index and Reality

4.1: One Shot Concepts

INTRODUCTION

A close look at the developments in India after independence brings us to the realisation that establishment of democracy – economic development coupled with the idea of distributive justice has transformed a traditional society. The state has been the central instrument of change. Politics has performed the role of an agent in facilitating this transformation. When India set out on its journey as an independent nation, in spite of our claim of being a democratic republic the political participation was constrained by social and economic inequalities.

Nevertheless, periodic elections at national, state and local levels have encouraged vigorous participation of traditionally suppressed and deprived sections of society. It can be said that democracy has proved to be a weapon against the privileges and powers of the few. Social and economic changes have gone a long way in relaxing the grip of rigid hierarchical structures, social discrimination and cultural attitudes. In spite of these positive developments India still has to contend with mass poverty, illiteracy, communal violence and atrocities against women.

SOCIAL REFORMS AND INEQUALITIES DURING COLONIAL PERIOD
Book Q.1

The social reform movements of the nineteenth century attacked caste system, which was graded into hierarchy of status. At the bottom of this caste system were placed the untouchables who constituted nearly twenty five per cent of the Hindu population and suffered the worst form of discrimination. They were not allowed to enter temples or to use tanks, wells and irrigation canals used by the higher castes. They could not go to schools in which children of upper castes studied. Entry to the public services like police or army was banned for them. The only option before them was of entering the menial jobs considered to be unclean like scavenging, removing dead bodies, etc. In some parts of the country even their presence was considered polluting.

Among the social movements mention must be made of some of them such as the one led by Jyotiba Phule in Maharashtra and Sri Narayan Guru in Kerala. These movements questioned the caste system and caste-based inequality. Gandhi made abolition of untouchability an integral part of the freedom movement. He made efforts to make the upper castes realise the enormity of injustice done through the practice of untouchability. He opposed British attempt to treat untouchables as separate from the Hindus.

B.R. Ambedkar who belonged to Mahar caste, an untouchable caste, in Maharashtra emerged as a powerful leader of the untouchables in the late 1920s. He fought against caste system and was in favour of separate electorate for the untouchables. His argument was that socially segregated should be politically segregated. When in 1932 the Communal Award provided for separate electorate Gandhi went on fast against it. Ambedkar agreed to sign the Poona Pact according to which untouchables were given reserved seats within the general Hindu category.

THE IDEA OF SOCIAL TRANSFORMATION IN THE WAKE OF INDEPENDENCE

Several members of the Constituent Assembly were of the view that the values and institutions of liberal democracy would transform India's tradition-bound social structure. Austin is of the view that the members of the Constituent Assembly opted for the Westminster model of liberal democracy. A liberal model of democracy based on the ideas of individual choice, consent, liberty and equality was seen as a liberating alternative to the old traditional organisation of life based on customs, ascriptive status, hierarchy and inequality. According to Austin it was also because of our familiarity with the working of these institutions under the colonial period. The Preamble of the Constitution promises to secure to all its citizens justice social, economic and political.

Liberal Democracy was found only in those countries whose economy was predominantly capitalist. What took place in these societies was democratisation of liberalism and liberalisation of democracy. The emphasis on economic justice as stated in the Preamble and through various provision of the Directive Principles of State Policy attempted to allay the bias of liberal democracy towards economic inequality. Members of the Constituent Assembly were optimistic about the potential of the democratic institutions provided by the constitution to transform Indian society.

At the time of independence the Indian state was being run by an elite political class which was primarily made of upper caste males. They also had preeminence of urban English educated Brahmins who shared secular outlook. The government under the Congress Party was a continuation of the British rule because like the British it did not attempt to change the social order but to adapt to it. Attempt by the parliament and the Congress Party to provide for economic social and educational upliftment of the underprivileged sections have largely been symbolic. The Congress Party adopted a conciliatory approach to the privileged and did not show much interest in organising poorer section of society for political action.

PEOPLE'S MOVEMENTS AS REFLECTION OF DEMOCRACY AND SOCIAL CHANGE
Book Q.2

The 1970s represents a watershed development. Indira Gandhi was attempting to strengthen the popular base of the state by a series of measures like bank nationalisation, abolition of privy purses and nationalisation of insurance. Policies targeting specific groups like SCs, STs, rural poor and workers were also made with the same objective. Indira Gandhi appealed directly to the vast masses of the rural and urban poor whose conditions had not improved even after three decades of independence. The appeal to this group and the slogan of Garibi Hatao translated in to electoral victory for the Congress Party led by Indira

Gandhi in 1971 General Election and the Assembly Election of 1972. By the beginning of 1973 Indira Gandhi started to decline.

People's expectations had remained unfulfilled. The policies of the government had failed to make dent in rural or urban poverty. The Congress Party was increasingly seen not as a party, which was interested in radical social change but as a party endorsing and reinforcing inequality. The country was faced with myriad problems like price rise, industrial stagnation, continuous failure of monsoons and large-scale unemployment. Agitations and protests were the order of the day. Poor peasant movements were going on in different parts of the country against the oppression of the landlords.

Firstly Gujarat and then Bihar became theatres of popular movements yearning for change. Jay Prakash Narayan popularly known as JP came out of political oblivion to lead the Bihar Movement and gave a call for Total Revolution. Very soon he took the movement outside Bihar. This movement received support from students, middle classes and a section of the intelligentsia.

BACKWARD CLASSES' AND DALITS' CHALLENGE TO THE DOMINANCE OF UPPER CASTES

The introduction of the universal adult franchise, periodic elections and of democratic consciousness led to forward caste dominance being challenged by first the middle castes and then by the dalits. Capturing power by the OBCs and dalits appears to be a panacea for the inequalities of status and income in-built in to the caste system. Laloo Yadav came to power by giving the slogan smash the upper castes [Bhura bal saf karo]. The prime concern of the leaders from these groups is gaining government positions.

Similarly, the BSP used slogans like mat hamara raj tumhara nahin chalega or vote se lenge PM/CM arakshan se SP/DM. They do not have faith in reforms. They aim at achieving social change not through social reforms but by share in political and administrative power. The Dalits and the other backward castes are by no means natural allies except for the fact that both these groups have been the victims of upper caste dominance and they stand to gain from the decline of this dominance. Between them they share a relationship of animosity, doubt and suspicion. There are instances of atrocities on dalits in many parts of the country by people belonging to other backward castes over question of wages, use of water from tanks or wells or other trivial matters.

STATE, DEMOCRACY AND CHANGE

In the north more particularly in the states of UP and Bihar state machinery, police, block development officer, village level workers and leadership of local Panchayati Raj Institutions were biased in favour of the rural rich. According to Ghanshyam Shah there existed a fraternisation between rural rich and bureaucracy. This was because most of the bureaucracy came from the same section of the society. The leadership of the political parties was also in the hands of the same section of society.

Caste	Book Q.3

The rise of the other backward castes movement and dalit movement has challenged the upper caste dominance. The complexion of national parliament and state assemblies has changed with more and more MPs and MLAs from these sections. The demand to implement reservation policy was not just for some jobs to unemployed youth from these sections of society but also for the crucial role they play in delivery of public funds. When Mayawati became Chief Minister she replaced upper caste officials holding key posts like chief secretary, CM's private secretary with scheduled caste officers. The same thing happened in Bihar with Laloo Yadav's rise in power where the upper caste officers were replaced by those belonging to the OBCs. The reservation of seats in the Panchayati Raj Institutions (PRIs) for SCs, STs and women provided by 73rd amendment can work as a bulwark against these organisations being manipulated for the benefit of the rural rich only.

Among the important programmes launched by Mayawati during her Chief Ministership was Ambedkar village development scheme providing development funds to 15000 Ambedkar villages with thirty per cent dalit population. But the dalit and backward class assertion is concentrating more on status and dignity and less on economic inequalities. Erecting statues of the non-Bramhin leaders like Jyotiba Phule, Periar/EV Ramaswamy Naicker, Ambedkar and Sahu Maharaj and installation of Ambedkar statues in every village and town were meant for fighting upper caste hegemony and boosting the status of the dalits.

In Tamil Nadu the politics of accommodation followed by the Dravida Munnetra Kazhagams has not caused much disturbance although the level of reservation has risen to 68 per cent including fifteen per cent for scheduled castes. The government provided opportunities for people from the lower castes in government jobs. The upper castes excluded from government jobs had no reason to sulk because they were encouraged to run privately founded engineering and medical colleges. These institutions were sustained by capitation fees charged from the students and were affiliated with state universities.

Gender

Dramatic changes have taken place in the status of women since independence. The constitution promised complete equality to women. Women like men also got right to vote. B.R. Ambedkar, the law minister after independence submitted a bill that raised the age of consent and marriage, upheld monogamy, gave women right to divorce, maintenance and inheritance and treated dowry as stridhan or woman's property. This bill faced stiff opposition from the conservative section of society. The bill had to be postponed because of this. Finally important sections of the bill got passed in four separate acts: The Hindu Marriage Act, the Hindu Succession Act, The Hindu Minority and Guardianship Act and the Hindu Adoption and Maintenance Act.

In 1985 the Supreme Court granted a pittance to Sahsp Bano, a divorced Muslim Woman; the conservatives among Muslim community created so much of furor in the name of interference in the Muslim personal law that Rajeev Gandhi's government wilted and introduced a bill in the parliament to negate the Supreme Court judgment. Some legal rights have been exercised even as some have remained on paper. The right to vote has been taken seriously by women even in rural areas. Many times they take free decisions independent of their husbands about whom to vote. The 73rd and 74th Constitutional Amendment Acts have provided for reservation of 33 per cent seats in local self-government institution both urban and local for women.

LIBERALISATION, POVERTY AND SOCIAL CHANGE   Book Q.4

Although the major Indian political parties contrived to mobilise the poor on the basis of community and not class, this does not mean that economic differentiation has ceased to be criteria to understand Indian politics. Except in Kerala and West Bengal the unorganised majority of the poor peasantry, agricultural labour, artisans and workers in informal sectors have become dependent on social welfare programmes sponsored by the central government. Even the redistributional programmes introduced in the early 1970s at the height of the Garibi Hatao campaign could not make any significant impact because of lack of commitment. In the 1990s the state in India has embarked upon the path of liberalisation. It was partly a response to depleting foreign exchange reserve and partly under pressure from world financial institution namely World Bank and IMF. The Indian state capitulated under pressure from western financial institutions into policy formation and running of state. Liberalisation is primarily beneficial to upper and middle classes.

The imperatives of economic liberalisation are identified with an aggravation of conflict between economic and political interest of the disadvantaged. Liberalisation is creating avenues for business and white-collar jobs to I.I.T and I.I.M. professionals. This suits the interests of the upper and middle class because they have the wherewithal like capital to benefit from new business opportunities opening up as part of liberalisation package. The youth from this section are more likely to walk away with jobs in Multi National Corporations with astronomical salaries because of their access to quality education. With privatisation and disinvestments becoming order of the day the number of jobs in public sector are going to be less and less.

4.2: IGNOU Book Exercise – Solved

1) Discuss how the social reforms and inequalities were related during the colonial period.

Answer by India Ebook: Read the 1 Shot Concept Above.

2) Write a note on the relationship between the peoples' movements and social change.

Answer by India Ebook: Read the 1 Shot Concept Above.

3) Explain the changes in Indian society with reference to the caste.

Answer by India Ebook: Read the 1 Shot Concept Above.

4) Write a note on the impact of liberalisation on the changes in Indian society.

Answer by India Ebook: Read the 1 Shot Concept Above.

4.3: IGNOU Past 6 Attempts Question – Solved

June 2021: Examine the impact of economic liberalization in Indian society.

Answer by India Ebook: Same as **Q.4** above.

5. GLOBALISATION AND SOCIAL MOVEMENTS

Introduction
Meaning of Globalisation
Impact of Globalisation
Globalisation, Social Movements and Developing Countries
Globalisation and Social Movements in India
> Farmers
> Working Classes
> Middle Classes
> Women
> Networking and Cooperation

5.1: One Shot Concepts

INTRODUCTION

Globalisation has brought profound transformation in the lives of people everywhere and it has immense potential to affect social, political and economic conditions globally. The critics of globalisation look at it as a process that can increase disparities of wealth and power. They are of the view that economic liberalisation is exacerbating the gap between rich and poor virtually in all developing regions. Globalisation has empowered some countries more than others. Rules and norms about investment, environmental management and social policy are made by these countries because they have power to control international institutions.

Globalisation is also transforming people's definitions of selfhood and identity. It is also averred that it has an inherent bias in favour of the middle class and hurts the interests of the underprivileged in material sense. The phase of globalisation has been charged with being a phase of jobless growth. The labour sector has witnessed retrenchment, voluntary retirement schemes and casualisation of workforce. The labour reforms that seem to be accompanying globalisation process seem to hurt the interests of workers at least in immediate sense. As part of conditions of **General Agreement on Tariffs and Trade** (GATT) signed at Maracas developing countries including India are being pressurised to keep the subsidies to farmers up to ten per cent of their value output. It has also introduced a patent regime. These developments have potential to affect Indian agriculture and the interest of the farmers in a fundamental sense.

MEANING OF GLOBALISATION

An important aspect of globalisation is state-led centralised and planned economic development being replaced with market led liberalised and globalised economic development. There seems to be disillusionment with the state and it is seen as source of all the evils and market is projected as panacea of all the economic evils.

Dreze and Sen are of the view that expansion of market is among the instruments that can help to promote human capabilities, and given the need of eliminating endemic deprivation in India it would be irresponsible to ignore the opportunity. State seems to be on the retreat. Even in India the state-centric developmental approach has come in for sharp criticism. The central role assigned to state and its bureaucracy in developmental projects has precluded participation of masses and local people in solving their problems.

The movements of international capital along with expansion of information technology have resulted in the erosion of the boundaries and sovereignty nation-sates. This void caused by the retreating state necessitates a dialogue between globalisation and social movements. Social movements have succeeded in conveying a message clearly that any developmental paradigm not providing for their participation will not be acceptable to them. In India initial doubts and apprehensions about globalisation seem to have waned. There seems to be greater consensus in favour of globalisation today.

IMPACT OF GLOBALISATION   Book Q.2

Indian economy was not an exception to this general pattern. The 1990s saw these countries launched on the path of privatisation, liberalisation and deregulation. India was also one of these countries. A combination of factors both international and national influenced India's decision to follow what came to be known as the New Economic Policy. India was faced with severe depletion of foreign exchange reserve. There was not enough foreign exchange reserve even to pay for imports of two months. The country was left with no option but to approach the World Bank and IMF for loans to avert the crisis.

To avail these loans the country had to agree to a package of Stabilisation and Structural Adjustment Programme. This package gave the muchneeded boost to the process of economic liberalisation in India. This gave an opportunity to the reform–oriented bureaucracy inside the government to go ahead with their long cherished agenda. The impending financial collapse firmed up the resolve to reform at the governmental level. The ideological opposition to the policy of reforms appeared to be weakest around this time. The economic policy Margaret Thatcher in England and Ronald Regan in America represented what came to be known as rolling back the state.

Jean Dreze and Amartya Sen are of the view that government policy at this time seems to be overwhelmingly concerned with removing counter–productive regulations. The state has been neglecting positive activities earlier also and continues to do so even now.

In India social movements have played an important role both before and after independence. Globalisation seems to be throwing newer challenges before social movements.

GLOBALISATION, SOCIAL MOVEMENTS AND DEVELOPING COUNTRIES

In the era of globalisation social movements all over the world have been active in ameliorating the conditions of people by launching movements against both democratic and undemocratic states. Some movements have taken advantage of the opportunities offered by globalisation for creating international networks. At the same time some movements have been busy fighting the negative effects of globalisation.

For the vast number of developing countries high growth economic activities propelled by globalisation pose serous threat to their environment and these activities may also lead to faster depletion of their resources. Globalisation has started a competition among the governments of the developing countries to create better investment climate. Many times this also means relaxing environmental safety guide -lines for attracting foreign investment. It is obvious that environment safety norms are compromised in the name of higher economic growth. This kind of growth has led to exploitation of Chile's native old-growth forest, the massive expansion of shrimp aquaculture in Honduras with the destruction of mangrove ecosystem. It also led to extraction of minerals on the scale of Brazil's Cajaras scheme.

All this exploitation of renewable and non- renewable resources has a common aim — generating export earning. In parts of India environmental pollution has reached disastrous proportion. Both the major rivers the Ganga and Yamuna have become polluted and the major cause of pollution is disposal of untreated industrial waste into these rivers. In places like Vapi, Ankleswar, Nandesari and Baroda in Gujarat the victims of pollution from factories and industries complain about holes in their clothes, death of buffaloes or elephants by drinking polluted water released in rivers, ponds or open spaces or farmers complain about crop destruction due to the pollution. The polluting industries refused to accept any responsibility.

GLOBALISATION & SOCIAL MOVEMENTS IN INDIA　Book Q.3

➤ Farmers

Globalisation is likely to have serious implications for Indian agriculture. India signed the General Agreement on Tariffs and Trade [GATT] at Maracas in 1994 and became part of the World Trade Organisation [WTO]. As part of the GATT agreement developing countries including India are under obligation to introduce reduction in subsidies and keep it to the 10 per cent of farmers' value output. But cutting down on subsidies does not seem to be practical because of strong resistance of the farmers' lobby. India together with other countries of the third world has accused the WTO of following discriminatory practices because the developed countries continue to give subsidies while they continue to pressurise the developing countries to cut subsidies. Another GATT–related problem affecting the interest of the farmers is introduction of patenting in agriculture. A farmer is not automatically permitted to use seeds of the protected varieties which he saved for sowing next crop.

➤ Working Classes

Globalisation has thrown big challenges before the working class movement. An important part of the globalisation agenda has been privatisation of public sector units in India, which has meant disinvestments from, and privatisation of the public sector enterprises.

Among the main planks of the New Economic Policy are closure of sick and loss making public enterprises. Workers have faced the prospect of retrenchment.

> Middle Classes

On the job front the complete story is not so dismal because globalisation has also unfolded big opportunities for lots of people, particularly of the upper middle class. This is especially true about people having degrees from the famous IITs and IIMs who are in big demand both in India and the world over.

Thus the introduction of the new economic policy has marginalised a large section of the population, as they do not have the necessary skills to benefit from the opportunities offered by globalisation. To make the marginalised partners in the bounty offered by globalisation process there is need of big investment in imparting that kind of skills in them that they do not lag behind aspirants from privileged section of society.

> Women

Globalisation can be seen as an ideology committed to production for profit, which leads to relative or absolute deprivation of women, colonies and marginal groups and communities. The suppression of women from participation in social, political and economic life hurts the society as a whole, not just women. Women have often been active in demanding and working for basic social change. Social movements in general and women's movement in particular should exert enough pressure on government so that proper policies for women's emancipation should be made and also implemented.

> Networking and Cooperation

Most of the social movements are generally preoccupied with their on particular struggle. They are gripped with the mindsets of "our movement" and "their movement". This exclusiveness makes them vulnerable in the event of oppression unleashed by state. With networking and coordination among them these social movements can play important role in achieving democratic social transformation. The need of networking and coordination is not limited to social movements within a country. Environment Movements and anti–WTO movements have demonstrated global networking and coordination.

5.2: IGNOU Book Exercise - Solved

1) Identify the main features of globalisation.

Answer by India Ebook: The following are the main features of Globalisation:

(i) Free Trade – Globalisation has helped improve trade volumes between nations with minimal interference. The reason is that governments are not micromanaging every minute aspect of business transactions. The Gross Domestic Product (GDP) of countries that have accepted globalisation has also increased significantly, thus bringing in greater prosperity. It has also resulted in better cooperation between governments that leads to further improvement in trade.

(ii) Liberalization – One of the main characteristics of globalisation is the improvement in the business climate for corporations. It has helped entrepreneurs to set up businesses and transact both within and outside the country. The rules and regulations for companies are relaxed significantly to allow for more trade between nations due to globalisation. Flexibility in trade regulations pushes governments to make further concessions to industries. Both Liberalization and Globalisation are dependent on each other.

(iii) Increase in Employment – Every industry is responsible for generating both direct and indirect jobs. And when production increases, it has a positive effect on employment. Globalisation helps companies increase their production capacity and set up operations in different parts of the world.

(iv) Interdependence – With the advent of globalisation, countries have become more reliant on each other. Businesses get the opportunity to import cheaper raw materials to produce their commodities. They are also being allowed to export to countries that have more demand for their finished goods. It has helped reduce trading barriers and build overall economic prosperity.

(v) Cultural Exchange – Improvement in people to people contacts have encouraged the intermingling of cultural practices and customs. It has allowed people to exchange ideas, behaviours and values with other countries. Communities are less isolated as a result of globalisation. For example, several American eateries have penetrated different parts of the world. Similarly, cuisine from far off countries is now readily available in the United States.

(vi) Production Cost – In a globalized world, companies are free to establish their operations in areas where the cost of production is low. The cheap availability of land, labour and raw materials has become very important. So it makes sense for companies to go where these resources are present in abundant quantities and at discounted rates. It helps them gain over their rivals by lowering costs and improving profit margins.

(vii) Outsourcing – One of the characteristics of globalisation is that it allows companies to bring in third parties from outside the country to manage specific processes. They take this step to reduce internal costs, improve the quality of services or both. Outsourcing is a boon for several human resource-rich countries that are looking to generate employment. Countries like India and the Philippines have benefitted immensely as a result of this practice.

2) Discuss the impact of globalisation on various sections of Indian society.

Answer by India Ebook: Read the 1 Shot Concept Above.

3) How do you relate the social movements to the impact of globalisation?

Answer by India Ebook: Read the 1 Shot Concept Above.

5.3: IGNOU Past 6 Attempts Question - Solved

June 2020: Evaluate the impact of information technology and globalization on social movements.

Answer by India Ebook: Same as **Q.3** above.

Dec 2020(Feb21): Examine the impact of globalisation on social movements in India.

Answer by India Ebook: Same as **Q.3** above.

Dec 2021: Assess the impact of economic globalization on Indian society.

Answer by India Ebook: Same as **Q.2** above.

NOTES

____
____
____
____
____
____
____
____
____

6. STATE, MARKET AND SOCIAL MOVEMENTS

Introduction
Changing Status of the Indian State
  ➢ State in the Post-Independence Period
  ➢ Discourse on the Indian State
Changing Status of the Market
State and Market in the New Context
Contextualising State, Market and Social Movements

6.1: One Shot Concepts

INTRODUCTION

With changes in the society and economy of India the number of social groups taking recourse to collective action increases. Their emergence has coincided with the latest phase of the globalisation, changing statuses of the state and market. These developments have given rise to debate in the academic and political discourse about the relationships between state, market and social movements. These also have generated a debate about the changes in the nature and roles of the state and market. The debate raises some questions.

- Has the nature of social movements changed or is changing with the expansion of market?
- What kinds of new social movements are emerging?
- Has the state become week and withdrawn from its responsibility for social transformation?
- Do the market forces dominate and govern the state?
- Are social classes getting fragmented and loose in their capacity to organise and dominate?
- Has class base of the social movements declined with the rise of market?

CHANGING STATUS OF THE INDIAN STATE   Book Q.1

➢ State in the Post-Independence Period

The trajectory of state in India during post-Independence period can be divided in two phases for the purpose of understanding its relationship to the market and social movements. These are — pre-1990s and post-1990; the phase preceding the present form of liberalisation and the phase coinciding with it. The pre-1990s phase can further be sub-divided into the era of dominance or autonomy of the state, identified with the Nehru-Mahalanobis model of development of the 1950s and mid-1960s and the phase between late 1960s and 1980s.

During the first two decades following Independence, the state was given a dominant place in the development model. The division of the country into India and Pakistan, the consequent communal riots, influx of refugees after partitions, merger of 565 princely states into the Indian Union, the division of the world in two ideologically opposite blocks — the American and Russian known to be involved in the cold war were the conditions which motivated the national leadership to adopt a development model in which the state would find a dominant place. Founded at the initiative of the then Prime-Minister Jawaharlal Nehru and P.C. Mahalanobis a development economist, this model which gave prominence to the state was known as **Nehru-Mahalanobis model** of development. The most forceful and effective intervention of the state in the rural economy was in the 1960s through the green revolution the HVY (High Yielding Varieties of seeds), fertilizers and inputs, seeds, machenisation, etc. in the selected areas of the country.

The period from the *late 1960s till the 1980s* saw the deinstitutionalisation and personalisation of the state machinery, specially during the **reign of Indira Gandhi**. With some interruption, this phase continued till the 1980s. This included period of emergency, more than four years' rule at the centre by different non-Congress political formations — the **Janata Party**, the Janata Dal government and the governments headed by Charan Singh and Chanra Shekhar.

The post 1990 phase, i.e., the era of **liberalisation** from the 1990s, has seen the decline in the state authority following the introduction of Structural Adjustment Programme introduced by the **Narasingha Rao government in 1991**. This phase is marked by the parallel rise of the market force, civil society organisations which have eroded the monopoly of the state.

> **Discourse on the Indian State**

Two perspectives have been followed to analyse the Indian state — its nature, autonomy and efficacy. These are Marxian and the non-Marxian.

The latter can further be sub-divided into development/ modernisation/ systemic and neo-liberal perspectives. The Marxian perspective is followed by academicians and different communist parties. The Non-Marxian scholars include the developmentalist / Modernists/ Behaviouralists like Rajni Kothari and Morris Jones and neo-liberals like P.N. Bhagwati, Srinivasn, Padma Desai, V K Ramaswami and B R Shenoy.

CHANGING STATUS OF THE MARKET — Book Q.2

The market was given secondary position in the policy formulations in relation to the state in the pre-liberalisation phase. The market not only had to depend on the state leadership and bureaucracy for clearance, licenses or operate under the inspector raj, it also had no major role in measures meant for various sections of the society. Besides, the market had to face the corruption/lack of transparency, redtapism, etc. These were in general taken to be failure of the state. This brought to the prominence the role of the state in the process of democratisation, governance and development.

This was a general trend world over. The western world with the neo-liberal ideology and through the institutions like the World Bank, International Monetary Fund, etc., played a leading role to propagate the ideas that the panaceas to the problems of the third world could be found if the state in these countries "rolled back" or became a minimalist state and structural reforms were introduced in these countries.

In case of India, by the 1980s the financial problems, mainly the balance of payment had become very acute. The solution to this was to be found in borrowing from the international donor agencies. But they could lend only if their conditions were accepted. As a result of this conditionality, government of India had to introduce the Structural Adjustment Programme which came to be known as — liberalisation, privitisation and globalisation. In India the present phase of globalisation or encouragement to the market started by the government led by P.V. Narasingha Rao in 1991. Despite opposition to the encouragement to the market — globalisation, different governments in India both at the centre and in the states have been pursuing globalisation since then.

The structural reforms in a sense became euphemism for the market. The indicators of this were: removal of tariff and non-tariff barriers within and outside the country; creation of the free economic/trade zones; dismantling the license system or the inspector raj; encouraging the private capital and discouraging the state/public capital or public sector units (disinvestments); allowing foreign capital or the multinational companies to invest in India and start their business operations here (allowing the FDI in different sectors of the economy). The market is also accorded priority in welfare sectors like education, health and setting up the infrastructure, etc.

Like in the case of the success, failure and nature of the state, the reaction to the market is also divided. If there are supporters of the market forces, there are also opponents of it. The latter include diverse forces — the leftists intellectuals and organisations, swedeshi (opposed to the foreign markets), and section of dalit spokespersons, a section of environmentalists, etc.

STATE AND MARKET IN THE NEW CONTEXT

The changes in the statuses of the state and the market have occurred in a new context. The features of this context are: decline of the cold war and disintegration of the socialist block in the 1980s and rise of civil society organisations, intellectuals, NGOs and Voluntary organisations. These developments resulted in the erosion of the monopoly of the state as the principal agency of working for the welfare of the society. Apart from the market, the new agencies in terms of civil society came to acknowledged as the potential agencies of welfare of the people. While the questions about the efficacy of the state and market whether one is more important than the other, continue to be debated, the significance of the civil society organisations has become enormous through out the world. The questions whether the NGOs alone can deliver the goods to people or they have do so in collaboration with state and market are being raised.

The growing significance of the civil society, existing along with the state and market, working either independently of or in collaboration with them, has become one of the principal focus of academic discourse and political activism. Along with civil society, the concept like the social capital have also come to occupy important place in the academic discourse. Existence of civil society, social capital and social movements are considered to be indicative of the existence of democracy in a section of the contemporary discourse.

CONTEXTUALISING STATE, MARKET AND SOCIAL MOVEMENTS

Book Q.3

Like on the statuses of the state and market, there are also opposite opinions on the relationship between the globalisation and social movements. The relationship of the social movements with the state and market can at best be seen in the following way: the state's ability to meet the aspirations of the people and their representation in the state agencies or organs, and with the market also its ability to give the people what the state has been unable to do. Different sections of people started questioning the model of development and nationstate building within a few years of implementation of the Constitution. There were movements on the ethnic, linguistic, caste and class issues. The personalisation of the state institutions by the political executive along with the growing corruption resulted in the Nav Nirman movement in Gujarat and JP movement known as Total Revolution. But unlike the latter decades, the mobilisation of these movements was done by the political parties, mainly the opposition or the non-Congress parties.

While the mobilisation up to the 1960s had been done mainly by the political parties or the organisations related to them, since the 1970s the different social groups came to be mobilsed by the non-party or apolitical organisations, though in the due course of time they became political. *Gail Omvedt* terms such movements as the new social movements as they share some characteristics which are new. The issues raised by these movements are related both to the state and market. They are related to the state as the state has been held responsible for neglecting them and thus forcing them to launch social movements. They are related to the market because of nature of their demands. The market-related demands are: the remunerative prices of the produce of the farmers, availability of the subsidised inputs.

The intervention of the market forces, especially the multinational organisations to appropriate the natural resources like water by the soft drink making companies has caused the movements of farmers in Kerala and Rajasthan against the usage of the ground water. Retrenchment of workers in several public sector undertakings, following their privatisation or closure, increase in the FDI in the Insurance and Telecome Companies has caused resentment in the working classes and the government employees. These, however, have not resulted in the sustained collective action.

From the 1990s onwards the issue of reservation in the private sector has also been added to the agenda of dalit leaders and political organisations. They apprehend that privatisation as a part of the globalisation will result in the reduction of the government jobs. This will harm the cause of social justice. They argue that in the light of the shrinkage of government jobs following the privatisation, reservation should be provided to dalits in the private sector.

6.2: IGNOU Book Exercise – Solved

1) Discuss the changing status of state in India.
Answer by India Ebook: Answer is *marked* in 1 Shot Concept Above.

2) Discuss the changing status of the market and analyse its relationship to the state in India.
Answer by India Ebook: Answer is *marked* in 1 Shot Concept Above.

3) How do you relate state, market and social movements to each other? Explain.
Answer by India Ebook: Answer is *marked* in 1 Shot Concept Above.

6.3: IGNOU Past 6 Attempts Question – Solved

June 2019: Discuss the changing nature of Indian society.
Answer by India Ebook: Almost same as **Q.6** above.

NOTES

____

____

____

____

____

7. DALIT MOVEMENT

Introduction
Who are Dalits?
Political Mobilisation of the Dalits
> Pre-independence Period
> Post-independence Period
Bahujan Samaj Party and the Dalits
> Ideology
> Limitations of the BSP

7.1: One Shot Concepts

INTRODUCTION

In recent years there has been a growth of academic interest in dalit mobilisation and movements in India. This is mainly due to the fact that there has been greater mobilisation and political participation of dalits in the electoral process in the country as a whole. It is primarily the **Bahujan Samaj Party (BSP)** which in fact is responsible for the mobilisation of the dalits and the democratic upsurge revolving around the dalits in the country.

WHO ARE DALITS? Book Q.1

The term 'dalit' is a **Marathi** word and literally means *'**ground**'* or *'**broken to pieces**'* and it was first popularised by the Dalit Panthers in Maharastra by which they meant the Scheduled Caste population. Later on there had been attempts to broaden this definition to any oppressed group (Chandra, 2004). Dalits generally refer to the Scheduled Castes alone, the castes that in the Hindu Varna system were outside the Varna system and were known as Avarnas or Ati-shudras. They were considered as impure and untouchables and were placed in the caste hierarchy which perpetuated inequality. There are even some people who include the Scheduled Castes, Scheduled Tribes, the Other Backward Classes and even other converted minorities into this category. The Dalits constitute around 16 per cent of the Indian population and belong to the lower rungs of the Indian society, economically and socially.

The Dalits not only belong to the lower caste category but also belong to the lower class category of the Indian society. They are mainly poor peasants, share-croppers and agricultural labourers in the rural economy. In the urban economy they basically form the bulk of the labouring population.

POLITICAL MOBILISATION OF THE DALITS

> Pre-Independence Period Book Q.1

At the All India level Ambedkar initiated the articulation of dalit interest for the first time in the 1920s. Prior to Ambedkar there had been attempts to bring about reforms in their condition in some of the Indian states, for example, Phule in Maharastra. But it was an attempt towards reform rather than towards the mobilisation of the dalits for political objectives. Ambedkar is known to have developed differences with Congress on several important questions relating to dalit issues and more or less remained the only spokesperson and the pre eminent advocate of the dalits from 1919, for more than three and half decades in the pre–independence period. Though the Congress talked about the necessity of removing untouchability, yet it did not articulate any concrete demand or programme to protect the interests of the depressed classes till 1917.

In contrast, mobilisation by Phule and Ambedkar in 1930s was firmly based on the belief that unless the caste system is destroyed the social evil of untouchability cannot end and that it is possible only if dalits acquire power. Hence in 1942 he formed the All India Scheduled Caste Federation (AISCF). Earlier he formed several organisations, the most important being the Indian Labour Party (ILP). The ILP was an organisation of a different kind in the sense that it aimed and attempted to mobilise a broader section of the Indian society and not exclusively the dalits.

➢ Post-Independence Period

The formation of the AISCF was a very significant development in the history of dalit mobilisation in the country though it was not much successful and suffered defeat in the elections of 1946 and again in 1951. The party, the first of its kind accepted the fundamental provisions of the Constitution and vowed to pursue its objective through the medium of parliamentary democracy. The RPI was also able to launch some major agitations for example, the agitations for land distribution in 1959 and 1964-65. These agitations, however, were more of an aberration rather than a general feature of RPI politics; they were, in fact, isolated episodes and not 'harbingers of sustained mass movements'. By the mid 1960s it had established itself in the state of Maharastra and Uttar Pradesh. These were the states in which it had a strong presence. Very soon, however, the RPI weakened largely because of internal differences on the issue of aligning with the Congress.

THE BAHUJAN SAMAJ PARTY AND THE DALITS   Book Q.2

The formation of the BSP by Kanshi Ram in 1984 marks a new beginning in the history of dalit mobilisation and politics in the country. The BSP succeeded at a time in north India when the dalit parties in western India were under disarray. The BSP after its formation has not only succeeded in establishing a stronghold in some states in northern India but it has also been able to form governments along with its pre or post electoral allies in the critically important state of Uttar Pradesh. The most important decision that was taken in the course of the formation of the BSP was the formation of Dalit Shoshit Sangharsh Samaj Samiti commonly known as the DS4 in 1981.

Having set the stage and the ground Kanshi Ram inaugurated the BSP on the 14th of April 1984. He acquired a useful partner when he persuaded Mayawati to join the party in Uttar Pradesh. The joining of Mayawati in Uttar Pradesh became crucial for BSP because with this the party was able to get a solid leader in the state. Mayawati belong to a Chamar family and studied in Meerut and Delhi Universities and was in the teaching profession. She left her job to become a full time politician. Her family was in fact associated with the RPI for some time in Uttar Pradesh.

➢ Ideology

The BSP ideology has to be understood in the background of the overall effort made towards mobilisation of the dalits since the national movement in India. It must be noted in the beginning that its ideology has been shifting from time to time according to its strategic needs. Gail Omvedt has noted that the BSP ideology can best be described as vague. She argues that there is no clear ideology in the programme and functioning of the party. The sole thrust is on the breaking of the caste system after acquiring state power (Omvedt, 1994). What is, however, true is that it has no economic programmes as such and hence the party is not clear what it intends to do after acquiring power. It is because of this ideological vagueness one finds that most of its agitations are symbolic in nature and it is not around economic issues. And secondly because of this it had vacillated on economic issues after acquiring power in the state of Uttar Pradesh.

Limitations of the BSP   Book Q.3

Now let us focus on the problems the limitations which the BSP confronts as a political party. We will see that the limitations the BSP faces are serious enough and some of these problems are similar to what the other Ambedkarite parties including the RPI had faced earlier.

One of the more serious problems, which it confronts, is the problem of ideology. It appears that the BSP has an exclusive ideology. It has a programme for the dalits in the country but not for the vast mass of the poor even though it claims that it represents the majority or the bahujans. Secondly, the ideological programme does not contain any economic programme for the category which it sought to mobilise. In the absence of an economic package or content the BSP ideology looks very limited, or restricted to social justice alone. That is why it has become difficult for the BSP to pursue or give directions to economic policies whenever it has attained power in the state of Uttar Pradesh. Thus the ideology of the BSP happens to be an exclusive one.

The second problem with the BSP, which Jagpal Singh (2002) and others have noted is that the BSP is a leader–centric party. Though it has adequate number of leaders and functionaries, yet it is a party in every sense led by its supremo Kanshi Ram and to some extent by Mayawati though in more recent times Kanshi Ram had been sidelined. On several important occasions it is these two important leaders who have taken decisions alone by ignoring the party altogether. This is a problem, which we have noted earlier, a problem common with the Ambedkarite parties formed after the death of Ambedkar.

The more serious problem with the BSP is its limited social base. Despite of all the talks of Bahujan Samaj and all the claims that the BSP will represent 85 per cent of the population in the Indian society the fact remains that in north India it remains a political party of Chamars/Jatavs. The Chamars constitute the backbone of the BSP support. We have seen earlier that the Chamars or the Jatavs in Uttar Pradesh were the most politicised of the castes in the state.

Fourthly, since the prime agenda of the BSP is to capture power and this had led the party to pursue unusual strategies to attain power in Uttar Pradesh. It had formed alliances with parties with which it does not have any ideological and programmatic affinity at all. Its alliance for example with BJP on three different occasions including during the 2002 elections has raised considerable doubts about the sanguine purpose and objective of the party.

7.2: IGNOU Book Exercise - Solved

1) Explain the meaning of "dalit" and discuss dalit mobilisation during the pre-colonial period.

Answer by India Ebook: Read the 1 Shot Concept Above.

2) Critically evaluate the growth, ideology and the social base of the Bahujan Samaj Party.

Answer by India Ebook: Read the 1 Shot Concept Above.

3) What are the limitations of the BSP? Discuss.

Answer by India Ebook: Read the 1 Shot Concept Above.

7.3: IGNOU Past 6 Attempts Question - Solved

Dec 2018: Discuss how far has the Dalit Movement realized its objectives.

June 2021: Discuss the political mobilization of Dalits since the 1980s.

Answer by India Ebook: Almost Same as **Q.1** above.

June 2021: Write notes (b) Bahujan Samajwadi Party

Answer by India Ebook: Same as **Q.2 & Q.3** above.

8. BACKWARD CLASS MOVEMENTS

Introduction

Who are the Backward Classes?

Socio-Economic Conditions of the Backward Classes: Impact of the State Policies

Backward Class Movement in the Post-Independence Period

> ➢ North-South Comparison
> ➢ The Electoral Mobilisation
> ➢ Politics of Reservation

8.1: One Shot Concepts

INTRODUCTION

Past three decades have seen the emergence of the backward classes in different fields of life. This has been more spectacular in electoral politics. Though backward classes became a significant social and political force in some parts of the country, especially south India even earlier, they got national attention following the introduction of the Mandal Commission Report by the V P Singh-led government at the centre in 1990.

WHO ARE THE BACKWARD CLASSES?

Marc Galanter in his book Competing Equalities: Law and The Backward Classes in India observes that backward classes is a very loose concept. Sociologically, these classes consist of a large number of the backward castes which remain above the Scheduled Castes and below the upper castes. These castes consist of intermediate castes — the cultivating castes, artisans and service castes. In the traditional social and economic structures, while the intermediary castes were involved in the production process in the land, the service castes and artisans provided services to the society. The backward classes known as the Other Backward Classes (OBCs), are other than those backward classes, which include the dalits/Scheduled Castes and the Scheduled Tribes.

The principal intermediary OBCs are Yadavs, Kurmies, Koeris, Gujjars and Jats in north Indian states like Uttar Pradesh, Bihar, Rajasthan and some of them in Haryana and Madhya Pradesh; Kappus, Kammas, Reddies, Vokkaliggas, Lingayats, Mudliars in south Indian states like Andhra Pradesh, Karnataka and Tamil Nadu; Patles, Kolis, Kshatriyas and Marathas in west Indian states like Guajarat and Maharashra. They belong to the upper or dominant backward classes. The service castes and artisans, principal castes among them being carpenters, blaksmiths, barbers, water carriers, etc., are found in almost all states in varying numbers. They are also known as the Most Backward Castes (MBCs) in some states.

To get categorised or recognised as an OBC, is political issue. A community should possess enough political clout to get itself identified as an OBC. There are several instances of demand by the castes to get themselves identified as OBCs. In 1999 the Rajasthan government and in 2000 the Uttar Pradesh government added the Jats to the lists of OBCs.

SOCIO-ECONOMIC CONDITIONS OF THE BACKWARD CLASSES: IMPACT OF THE STATE POLICIES

The backward classes emerged as a powerful social, economic and political block during the post-indenpendence period in the countryside as a result of the policies of the state. But there have remained internal differentiation among them. While the intermediary castes came to control the affairs of the village society, the artisans and the service castes joined the ranks of the marginalised groups of the wage labourers, marginal and poor farmers.

The principal policies which impacted them included: the land reforms which consisted of the abolition of landlordism, putting ceilings on the size of the landholdings, consolidation of landholdings, and Green Revolution in the selected areas of the country; welfare schemes

for the welfare of the lower backward classes. Besides, the state policies the changes which occurred from within the society — population growth, breaking down of the jajmani system also affected them. Although the state policies in different states of the country did not have the uniform and desired impact on the backward classes in the country, they definitely gave rise to the backward classes.

Another factor which is related to the changes in the socio-economic conditions of the backward classes is rise of a middle class among the OBCs. Despite the failure of the education policies a group of educated persons, who became their spokespersons, had emerged among the backward classes. However, this group was not as big as it was among the high castes. In north India Charan Singh, S. D. Singh Chaurasia and Chaudhry Brahm Prakash were some of the spokes persons of the backward classes belonging to the early decades following Independence.

BACKWARD CLASS MOVEMENT IN THE POST INDEPENDENCE PERIOD

> **North-South Comparison:** Book Q.2

In comparison to North India, the backward classes in south India were moblised much earlier. They not only got reservation in the government jobs but they were also mobilised into the social movement and entered politics in south India much before than the backward classes of North India. Through ethnicisation the backward classes of south India questioned the Brahminical domination and sought to replace it with that of the backward classes or dravidians. It was a revolt against sanskritisation in south. They not only got reservation in the public institutions and they replaced the brahminical domination in politics also. Scholars explain this difference between north and south in the following way. The Brahmins had monopolised the high castes domination over the low castes in South India and their number in comparison to Brahmins of north India was much smaller. In contrast, the Brahmins were not the only high castes in north India. Their domination over the low castes was shared, thus diluted, by several high castes - Rajputs, Kayasthas or even Vaishyas.

In north India the organisation like Arya Samaj spread the message among the backward classes that it was the karma not the birth which determined the place of a person in society. While it encouraged the backward classes to sanskritise themselves by tracing their lineages to the high castes, wearing janeo (sacred threads), etc., it also attempted to bring back to Hinduism those Muslims who were supposed to

have converted from Hindu religion through the Suddhi movement. This instead of challenging the hegemony of the high castes or Brahminism revived it and strengthened it. As a result it dampened the chances of strong backward class movement in north India.

The backward classes virtually were the non-Brahmin classes in south India. Unlike their counterparts in north India, they did not attempt to follow the high casts, i.e. Brahmins, they in fact questioned their domination in culture, administration and politics. The most effective expression of the dravidian revolt against the Brahmin domination in south was provided by the Self-Respect Movement led by E.V. Ramaswami Naicker, alias Periyar, during the 1920s and 1940s. The Self-Respect Movement was based on the premise that the original inhabitants of India were non-Brahmins or the dravidians, not the Brahmins. The main principle of this movement was Samadharma or equality. In order to get their self-respect and the non-Brahmins should replace the dominance of Brahmins in education, culture, politics and administration. The Self-Respect Movement included: boycott of Brahmins in rituals like weddings; condemnation of varnashrama dharma; burning of Manu Smriti.

> **The Electoral Mobilisation**   Book Q.3

The backward class politics in India has largely been related to electoral mobilisation and creation of support base among them by the political parties and leaders. Other issues like the reservation for the OBCs or their mobilisation on the class issues like those related to the farmers also get linked to the electoral politics. The increasing participation of the OBCs, their entry into the state legislatures and parliament is indicative of the empowerment of the backward classes. During the post-Independence period there have been attempts on the parts of individual leaders and political organisations to mobilise the backward classes into the participatory politics. While the backward classes in south India emerged before the independence and they benefited from this legacy in the post-Independence period, in the north India their systemic mobilisation took place in the post-interdependence period. The main leaders and political parties which mobilised the backward classes in north India include Charan Singh, Karpoori Thakur, Socialist parties and the different political formations at different point of times like Samajwadi Party and Rashtriya Janata Dal in Uttar Pradesh and Bihar.

Charan Singh carved out a political base for himself among the middle caste peasantry in UP and Bihar through a well designed strategy. He could do this while he was still a member of the Congress Party. Though Jats, the caste he belonged to did not fall in the official category of the OBCs till 2000 in UP and 1999 in Rajasthan, he identified himself with the backward classes of UP and Bihar. These castes were mainly Yadavas, Kurmies, Koeries, Kachhis, Lodhs, etc. His strategy was two fold — he combined the caste issue with the class issue.

Sanjay Kumar observes in his article "New Phase in Backward Caste Politics in Bihar, 1990-2000" (1999) that it was 1995 assembly election in Bihar which showed a new trend towards the empowerment of the OBCs in the state. It was marked by the polarisation of the backward support base; Yadavs supported the Janata Dal while the Kurmies and Koeries supported Samata Party. The fact remains that despite the division in their support to different parties including the BJP, the OBCs have become a force to reckon with in politics of Bihar. The division of support of backward classes to different parties is indicative to the competitive politics among the backward classes, to their empowerment. In case of Gujarat Ghanshyam Shah argues that the OBCs' support to BJP there does not mean their support to the ideology of "Brahminical dominance". It is "part of an electoral game" in which the needs of the upper backward classes are satisfied.

> **Politics of Reservation**   Book Q.4

The introduction of Mandal Commission Report by the V P Singh's government in 1990 recommending reservation 27 per cent reservation for the OBCs in the central government jobs made the reservation a national issue in Indian politics. It not only drew reactions in its support or against it, it also changed the contours of Indian politics. The appointment of Mandal Commission by the Janata Party government in 1990 was result of the pressure of the backward classes leadership and their clout. As mentioned earlier by the 1970s the backward classes, especially those belonging to the intermediate castes had already made their presence felt in the politics of India and states.

The demand for reservation for the backward classes was raised in the Constituent Assembly by Punjab Rao Deshmukh, like Dr. B.R. Ambedkar had raised the similar demand for the Scheduled Castes. In order to articulate the reservation issue for the backward classes he founded All India Backward Classes Federation (AIBCF) on 26 January 1950. Within the AIBCF the differences grew between those having allegiance to the Congress on the one hand and those having allegiance to the Socialist Lohiaites. This resulted in the split in the AIBCF, with the splinter group naming itself as National Backward Classes Federation (NBCF). The former was headed by Punjab Rao Deshmukh, a Congress leader and the latter was headed by R L Chandpuri. After the death of Chandpuri , Chaudhry Brahm Praksah became its leader. Besides, a large number of informal and unregistered organisations existed in different states and different levels in country.

The Mandal Commission was result of the consistent demand by the backward class leadership to get the Kaka Kalelkar Commission's, the first backward class commission report accepted. The Kaka Kalelkar Commission was also the result of the demand for such commission by the backward class leadership at the time of Independence. But Kaka Kalelkar's recommendations of class as the criterion for identification of the backward classes and rejection of the Commission's report by the parliament led to the demand of appointment of another commission which would take social and educational backwardness as the criteria for identification of the backward classes.

The implementation of the Mandal Commission report, however, has not settled the issue of reservation. Newer groups continue to demand to be recognised themselves as the OBCs. Whether a community can get itself identified as OBCs is a political question; it depends on the political factors.

8.2: IGNOU Book Exercise – Solved

1) Who are the backward classes? Discuss the impact of the state policies on their emergence.

Answer by India Ebook: Read the 1 Shot Concept Above.

2) Compare the conditions of the backward classes in north India with those in south India.

Answer by India Ebook: Read the 1 Shot Concept Above.

3) Discuss the patterns of mobilisation of backward classes in electoral politics.

Answer by India Ebook: Read the 1 Shot Concept Above.

4) Write a note on the reservation politics.

Answer by India Ebook: Read the 1 Shot Concept Above.

8.3: IGNOU Past 6 Attempts Question - Solved

June 2019: Evaluate with examples the impact of state policies on backward classes.

Answer by India Ebook: Same as **Q.1** above.

Dec 2021: Explain the economic impact of State policies on backward classes.

Answer by India Ebook: Same as **Q.1** above.

Dec 2021: Trace the origin of the Backward Classes Movement in India.

Answer by India Ebook: Same as **Q.1** above.

June 2020: Discuss the main features of Other Backward Class (OBC) Movement in India.

Answer by India Ebook: Refer Concept above.

Dec 2020(Feb21): What is the role of State in empowering the socially and educationally backward classes?

Answer by India Ebook: Refer Concept above.

NOTES

9. ETHNIC MOVEMENTS WITH SPECIAL REFERENCE TO TRIBALS

Introduction
What are Ethnic Movements?
Approaches to Study Ethnic Movements
Ethnic Movements During Post-independence Period: A General View
Ethnic Movements with Special Reference to Tribals
- ➢ Who are Tribals?
- ➢ Tribals of North-East India or the Frontier Tribes
- ➢ Tribals of Regions other than North-East India or the Non-frontier Tribes

9.1: One Shot Concepts

INTRODUCTION

Even before India could assume its present shape a sovereign, democratic and secular republic following the attainment of Independence from the British rule, different ethnic groups have been clamouring for their recognition in the society in terms of cultural, economy and politics. Such claims became more strident after the country became independent. As the time passes more and more claims are made by several groups, many of whom were not visible on the political scene earlier. Many scholars categorise such movements as ethnic movements.

WHAT ARE ETHNIC MOVEMENTS? Book Q.1

For a proper understanding of ethnic movements it necessary to understand what we mean by ethnicity as such movements are associated with it. Ethnicity is denotes towards identification of a group of people on the basis of certain criteria or markers which they are supposed to share with each other. These markers include culture, race, language, religion, customs, history, economic experiences, etc. For a group of people to share such attributes another requirement is that they get mobilised into some collective action for attainment of certain demands. The number of markers or attributes which form the basis of an ethnic group depends on the choice of these factors by the ethnic group or its leadership. But there are differences among the scholars regarding the number of attributes which constitute and ethnic group. Scholars in India generally consider that mobilisation as ethnic which is based on the multiple attributes — language, religion, culture, history, economy, etc. For example, the language based mobilisation is considered as linguistic mobilisation and the groups as such is considered as linguistic group.

Similarly caste based mobilisation is considered as dalit, backward or any other caste mobilisation. In India the religion-based mobilisation is called communal mobilisation. But the scholars who follow American and European traditions catergorise even the mobilisation based on the single attribute — language, religion, caste, etc, as ethnic mobilisation. They also do not distinguish between the communal and ethnic mobilisation.

APPROACHES TO STUDY ETHNIC MOVEMENTS   Book Q.1

The most commonly used approaches to study the ethnic movements are: the primorial, the instrumentalist and the approach which combines the features of primordial and instrumentalist approaches. The primordial approach holds that the basis of the formation of the ethnic groups are "given". There are traits of an ethnic group which are inherited by them, i.e., culture, language, customs, religions, etc. Similarly other ethnic group also has certain inherited characteristics.

The advocates of the instrumentalist approach on the other hand believe that ethnic groups are creation of the leadership or the elites belonging to these groups. The differences in the language, culture, customs, economic conditions of the people or the social cleavages are manipulated by the elite of the ethnic groups to generate ethnic consciousness and start ethnic movements. There both real and imagined reasons for the formation of ethnic movements and generation of the ethnic movements. The ethnic community when created on the basis of imagined attributes are thus "imagined" or "constructed" communities.

The advocates of the third approach believe that both of these approaches are marked into "bi-polarity" — the basis of ethnicity is either "given" or "imagined" or "constructed". But there are problems with both of these approaches. While the "primordial" approach does not explain why and how an ethnic group gets mobilised into the collective action, the "instrumentalist" approach does not explain as to why an ethnic group responds to the call of the elite, leaders or politicians. They advocate a combination of both the primordial and instrumentalist approaches instead of "bi-polar" approach.

ETHNIC MOVEMENTS DURING POST-INDEPNDECE PERIOD: A GENERAL VIEW   Book Q.2

Starting with the rejection of the Indian Constitution by the Nagas in the North-East, it spread in the form of Dravidian ethnic movement and demand for the formation of linguistic states with classic example of the movement of for creation of separate state of Andhra Pradesh in South, movements in Jammu and Kashmir and Punjab and Shiv Sena's against South Indians in Mumbai.

In Tamil Nadu following the legacy of E V Ramaswami Naicker three issues formed the basis of ethnic movement in the first two decades following independence – language, dravidian culture, and religion. The leadership of the movement argued that imposition of the North Indian Hindi language, Brahinical Hindu religion and Aryan culture were detrimental to the development of the dravidian identity. Therefore, the Tamil ethnic movement had demanded, stoping of the imposition of Hindi language secession from India. However, towards the end of the 1960s the demand for secession was given up by the Tamil nationality/ethnic group.

The ethnic movement in Punjab was based on three types of issues – regional, religious and economic. Spearheaded by the Akali Dal, the leadership in Punjab argued that since Sikhs follow a separate religion and speak different language, they should get a separate state. On some occasions, it got reflected in the communal divide between the Hindus and Sikhs in the state, resulting in the ethnic conflict. They launched a Punjabi Suba movement during the 1950s and 1960s demanding a separate state of Punjab for them. Baldev Raj Nayar observes that Akali Dal's strategy during the Punjabi Suba movement included constitutional means like memoranda, rallies and marches; penetration into the Congress organisation in order to influence the party in favour of a separate state; and, agitational means which included marches to shrines, intimidation and force. As a result of the Punjabi Suba movement, Punjab was created as separate state on November 1, 1966.

The ethnic movement in Punjab again arose in the 1980s. It challenged the sovereignty of the Indian state the notion of India as a nation-state. It sought to establish a sovereign state of Khalistan, to be based on the tenets of Sikhism. The Khalistan movement and the issues related to were generally referred to as "Punjab Crisis". The movement became violent and came to be identified with terrorism in the popular, academic and political discourse. The advocates of the Khalistan movement argued that Sikhs, as followers of the minority religion have been discriminated in India despite their contribution to Indian economy and army. The rise of Khalistan movement, terrorism or the in the 1980s has been a sequence to the political developments in the country which preceded it.

The basis of ethnic movement in Jammu and Kashmir are language, religion and geographical location. A section of people of the state have argued since the ethnic composition of state in terms of language, religion and geography is different from the dominant ethnic groups in the country, region should be treated differently. Some of them have not considered themselves as members of the Union of India. As a result, they have demanded cessation from India; some have advocated merger with Pakistan, some have demanded a separate state for the region and some have advocated merger of two Kashmirs — one occupied by Pakistan and other of India, to become a single state. Supporters of this perspective have launched insurgency involving violence and loss human beings and material. Hari Singh, the ruler of the Jammu and Kashmir initially opposed the accession of the state into the union of India. But he had to agree to it in the face of attack of the Pakistani forces. Sheikh Abdullah had supported the merger of the state with Union of India. He formed Plebiscite Front, which led to his incarceration by the central government from 1953 till 1964.

ETHNIC MOVEMENTS WITH SPECIAL REFERENCE TO TRIBALS

In fact, the tribals provide the most appropriate examples of the ethnic movements in the country. In their case, almost all factors, both real and imagined, which the tribal communities share among themselves – culture, customs, language, race, religion (indigenous or otherwise), economic issues, contribute to their mobilisation. Even if the their mobilisation starts with a single marker, it is the multiple markers which come to play their roles in the due course.

The most common issues which account for the tribals' ethnic mobilisation are: perceived or real threat to their indigenous culture and economy including the natural resources like mineral, forest and modern market opportunities by the outsiders (non-tribals middle classes, businessmen, moneylenders, bureaucrats); their discrimination by the state, especially at the central levels and its representatives (central government employees, army, police, etc.).

> **Who are Tribals?**

Unlike the Scheduled Castes, there are differences among the scholars on the criteria to identify the tribals or the Scheduled Tribes. While the Scheduled Castes consist of the erstwhile untouchable castes placed in the lowest rung of the Hindu society, the tribals follow multiple religions in the country – Buddism, Christianity, Islam or their indigeneous religions. However, there is almost unanimity among the scholars on certain characteristics of the tribals.

The principal of these **characteristics** are as follows:

1) Their close association with nature, mainly the forests;

2) Relatively traditional means of cultivation and less developed market;

3) Near absence of the rigid division within the community and discrimination on the basis of birth, unlike the caste division among the Hindus;

4) Presence of the traditional chiefs or headmen and better position of women as compared to the non-tribals;

5) Attachment/reverence to traditional customs and culture.

Article 342 of the Constitution attributes "isolation, backwardness and cultural distinctiveness" as the characteristics of the Scheduled Tribes.

These characteristics, however, have undergone changes as a result of modenisation – education, impact of Christianity on many tribes, changing cropping pattern or penetration of market, economic differentiation and emergence of middle classes and in some cases decline in the authority of the traditional chiefs. These changes have given rise to the ethnicisation of tribes reflected in their ethnic movements.

Article 342 mentions 212 Scheduled Tribes in the country. The tribes are found in all parts of the country – all states of north-east India, Madhya Pradesh, Orissa, Rajasthan, Jharkhand, Guajarat, Dadra Nagar Haveli and Lakshdweep Islands. The tribals of north-east are called frontier tribes and those of other parts of the country are called non-frontier tribes. Of the entire tribal population 11 per cent are found in north-east India and 89 per cent are found in other regions. Tribals have been involved in the collective action for one or the other goals.

> **Tribals of North-East India or the Frontier Tribes** Book Q.3

North-East India as a single region has the largest number of the tribal population in the country. They follow different religions especially Christianity, Budhism, Hinduism and indigenous religious tenets. They can further be divided between the plain and hill tribes. Almost all state of North-East India have witnessed one or the other forms of ethnic movements. In this sub-section we will deal with some ethnic movements with examples from states of North-East India – Nagaland, Assam and Meghalaya.

It is important to note ethnic issues of North-East India are related to the geographical factors, its regional dimensions. Though there are differences among different tribals of North-East India in terms of their cultural practices, they share common experience of deprivation due to their regional location. A large amount of literature exists on the North-East which seeks to explain the ethnic problems of the region. But there are wide differences in the discourse on explaining the ethnic issues of the region. And the divide in the discourse also reflect on the basis of the formation of the ethnic identities and the movements in the regions.

The problems of the North-eastern region – insurgency, autonomy movements, ethnic conflicts, riots, etc., have been explained by mainly two perspectives: first, the modernisation/development/"nation-state building" perspective and; second, the "federation-building perspective". The followers of the first perspective largely argue that the problems of the North-East are related to the issues of "nationstate building"; conflict between the new middle classes, especially among the tribals of the region, which has emerged as a result of the modernisation/development/transition Democratisation) with the traditional leadership; inability of the system to meet the rising aspiration of this group.

The second perspective is actually the critique of the first one and is available in the writings of the scholars who hail from the region. The principal adherents of this perspective are Sanjib Baruah, Udyan Sharma, Sanjay Hazarika, Sajal Nag, M P Bezbaruah. They argue that problems of the North-East India arose because the nation leadership overlooked the perspective of the people of the region in their quest for "nation-building". In order to build "nation-state" the central government adopted "step motherly" treatment towards the North-East; ignored the "periphery" and the smaller nationalities; shown arrogant attitude towards them; have been indifferent to the human rights violation in the region. They argue for a "Federation-Building" perspective in place on the "nation-state" building perspective.

The Nagas

Movement of the Nagas which is often referred to as Naga insurgency is called the Naga national movement by the Nagas. It is the oldest movements relating to the ethnicity or the nationality question in the country. The nationality/ethnicity in Nagaland had all dimensions relating to the ethnic movement – demand for autonomy, secession from India and ethnic conflicts. Nagas believe that they form a nation which is different from other ethnic groups or nationalities/nations in India. They had always enjoyed their sovereignty with distinct culture, customs and history.

Bodos of Assam

The tribals of Assam – Bodos, Karbis and Adivasis have been involved in collective ethnic mobilisation since 1980s. The Bodos and Karbis are demanding creation of the separate states respectively from within the present Assam. The Bodos and Karbis are the indigenous tribes inhabiting their respective habitats. The former are found in lower Assam districts like Kokhrajhar, and Karbis inhabit Karbi Anlong district of the state. The tribals of Assam participated in the six year long Assam agitation led by the **All Assam Students Union** (AASU) from 1989 to 1985. The movement which was directed against the foreigners united major communities of Assam — tribals and non-tribal Assamese, on the common perception they shared common experience in terms of their belonging to a backward and discriminated state, facing the challenge of the foreign infiltration, especially from Bangladesh and Assam.

Tribes of Meghalaya

Meghalaya has three main tribes – Khais, Jaintias and Garos, who inhabit Khasi, Jaintian and Garo hills of the state. They are distinct for the existence matrilineal system which accords better position to women as compared to the patrilineal found among other communities of India. Like some other tribes of the North-East India, educated Christian elite had already emerged among them in the state, especially the Khasis during the pre-Independence period. Shillong which remained capital for around a centurty of Assam, of which areas consisting present Meghalaya state were constituent, provided a suitable place for the growth of an elite section among them. The tribals of Meghalaya have been coexisting with non-tribals in Meghalaya, especially Shillong since the late 19th century, following shifting of the capital of Assam from Cherrapunjee to there. The nontribals who migrated into Shillong and other parts of Meghalaya since the late 19th century consist of mainly Bengalis, Biharis, Rajasthanis, Sikhs and till formation of Megalaya as a separate state in 1972, the Assamese. The non-tribals despite their differences form a separate ethnic groups in the sense that their culture, features, customs, etc. are different from those of the tribals.

> **Tribals of Regions other than North-East India or the Non-Frontier Tribes**   Book Q.4

The tribals of other regions than the North-East or the Frontier tribes of the states of Madhya Pradesh/Chhattishgarh, Bihar/Jharkhand, Gujarat, Rajasthan and several others states have been mobilised on ethnic lines on several occasions. In modern history their revolt had been conspicuous against the intervention of the British authorities in the power of the tribal chiefs and against exploitation of their natural resources by the British and their collaborators such as the outside businessmen and bureaucrats or dikus. The tribal chiefs mibilised their fellow tribals in order to restore their power and resources and evoked their golden past in order to retain their ethnic identity and autonomy. The British administration retaliated against these movements with ruthless violence including assassination of the leaders of these movements. **<u>Birsa Munda revolt</u>** in Chhota Nagpur was among the most prominent of such movements during the pre-Independence period. Such movements have been termed as **"millenarian movements"** by K S Singh.

The issues which formed the basis of collective mobilisation of the non-frontiers tribals in the post-independence period have varied from state to state. These have included the movements for creation of separate states for the tribals out of the existing states like Jharkhand out of Bihar and Chhattisgarh from Madhya Pradesh or separate districts within the same state like demand by the Dang tribes for creation of a separate state within former Bombay state; against the encroachment of tribal land for the creation of dams resulting in the displacement like in the Narmada Valley. Some scholars have observed that during the 1990s the tribals have been mobilsed by the Hindutva forces against the Christian and Muslim tribals in some states, especially Guajarat, Madhya Pradesh and Rajasthan. This contributed to the division of the tribals on the communal basis.

The movement for autonomy expressed in the form of demands for separate states, districts out of present states or creation of autonomous administrative bodies are among the most commonly raised demands of the tribal movements. The basis for such demands are their grievances against the dominant for political formations: their cultural and linguistic identities are under the threat of erosion; their economic resources and opportunities are appropriated by others/outsiders; they are not given due recognition, etc. The tribal leadership, both traditional and modern, mobilises the tribals into collective actions. The acceptance of their demands depends on the political circumstances. But once a set of demands is accepted, the leadership looks for other issues. For example, after the creation of separate state of Jharkhand out of Bihar, the tribal leaders attempted to change the domicile laws. Similarly, after the creation of a separate state of Meghalaya, the tribal leadership introduced legislation changing the rules regarding inheritance and transfer of land. Thus, the ethnic mobilisation is a continuous process in a democracy.

9.2: IGNOU Book Exercise – Solved

1) Explain the meaning of ethnic mobilisation and discuss the approaches to study it.

Answer by India Ebook: Read the 1 Shot Concept Above.

2) Give a general view of the ethnic mobilisation during the post-colonial period.

Answer by India Ebook: Read the 1 Shot Concept Above.

3) Discuss the general features of tribal ethnic movements in **North-East** India.

Answer by India Ebook: Read the 1 Shot Concept Above.

4) Write a note on the ethnic movements of the non-frontier tribes.

Answer by India Ebook: Read the 1 Shot Concept Above.

9.3: IGNOU Past 6 Attempts Question – Solved

June 2019: What are the approaches to study of ethnic movements?

Answer by India Ebook: Almost Same as **Q.1** above.

June 2021: What are the general features of ethnic movements in North-East India?

Answer by India Ebook: Almost Same as **Q.3** above.

Dec 2021: Describe ethnic movements in North-East India.

Answer by India Ebook: Almost Same as **Q.3** above.

NOTES

Introduction

The Colonial Context: The Vision of a New Society and the Reform Movement

> The Issue of Priority: Social or Political?
> Women's Issues During the Gandhian Era

The Post-Independence Period: State, Reform and Women

The Left and Women's Movements

Equality or Difference

New Social Movements

10.1: One Shot Concepts

INTRODUCTION

Like other social groups women also have been involved in collective actions equipped with their agenda, leadership, ideologies and organisations in order to have their proper and dignified place in all aspects of life. This unit deals with social movements of women. Women as individuals and as a group are among the most discriminated sections of world population. As a marker of this discrimination, societies across the world have shown preference for boy child. The preference for boy child has taken societies to the extent of killing girl child in the womb itself. All practices of discriminations in societies have been legitimised through either invoking socio-cultural needs or the need to maintain a lineage or for material production.

As the second sex in material terms means that women is quite often denied political, economic and even cultural rights. She quite often does not have right to inherit property along with her male siblings. She does not have either equal access to education and health care equal to a male counterpart. She is also perennially in the danger of being the target of male violence within the family or outside. Historically religion, polity and society have been so organised as to make her position vulnerable to any discriminatory trends in the society. There have been protests and revolts by people including women to question such discriminating arrangements within the society. Nationalist movement in the colonial countries, socialist and communist movement and feminist movement across the world and the larger trend of democracy have been some of the powerful streams that presented themselves as catalyst of change in this regard. In the increasingly globalising world women's issues and concerns are becoming increasingly part of the larger movements.

The relationship between women and social movements is quite intricate. First, one is not very clear as to where and how do women figure in the broad contour of different social movements. It has been found that women were merely part of the mobilised section of some movement whose overall objectives are detrimental to women's interests and concerns.

Second, related to the nature of social movement is: whether it allows the space for the articulation of issues and concerns regarding women. Indian national movement was one such movement whose democratic and secular character had given the space for many democratic movements to spring up and voice their concern. Women's movement in India is one such example where the contours of the movement coalesce with the mass phase of the Indian national movement. The notion of equality, idea of justice and democracy, central to the core of the movement of national liberation, were also the premises of the women's movement.

Historically, changing conditions of women and their status constituted the core of the social reform movement that began to take shape in the early decades of the nineteenth century. By the early decades of the twentieth century this core is enlarged by bringing two issues, i.e., equality of women in modern political, social and cultural realm, and women's role in the developmental process, into its ambit. Though the rapid changes in the society, economy and culture have led to rethinking on many issues, the social movements in the country more or less have directed their concerns about women along this core.

THE COLONIAL CONTEXT: THE VISION OF A NEW SOCIETY AND THE REFORM MOVEMENT Book Q.1

In India, like in many other colonised countries, it was colonialism in the 18th and 19th centuries that brought the new economic and political processes into operation. The coming of the British, the Christian Missionaries and their criticism of the Indian society presented a big challenge to the local intellectuals and social leaders. The former attacked the indigenous society and its treatment of women and the lower caste. It presented new organising principle, equality, or Christianity in some cases. It also brought blueprint for a new organising principle for the society. While colonialism as a system exploited the colonies and stunted its natural and potential growth, it brought, at the same time, the new ideas of democracy, idea of equality and justice.

The nineteenth century Hindu, Parsee, Muslim reformers took the challenge and first tried to reform their own societies in the face of such a massive criticism. Ram Mohan Roy, for example, while he attacked the missionaries for presenting distorted picture, was also preparing agitation against Sati and the customs of caste inequalities. In the later part of the century, reformers took the questioning of women's condition very prominently and all the major reform efforts aimed at ameliorating their conditions. Ishwar Chandra Vidyasagar made great efforts in getting widow remarriage society established. Similarly women's education too was thought to be one of the most important steps in this direction. Veereshlingam Pontulu, Jyotiaba Phule, Badruddin Tybaji, Dadabhai Naoroji all contributed greatly in this direction.

In the later part of the nineteenth century, when there was in some sense a reassertion of the racial and imperialist ideas, there were a movement among the Indians which tried and asserted its own historical superiority. In this line that they looked into the past to suggest that woman was in some sense better placed in those days than they were now. In this sense the problem of integrating women's question into the social movement become more intricate— if the situation became bad what should one do was the question that led to the major indicator of the movements' thrust. It was to the credit of the intelligentsia who fought the issue of social reform that the issue of women remained in the forefront. One of the most intensely fought issues was the between the social reformers and those who separated the social issues from the political fight.

> ### The Issue of Priority: Social or Political?

These have been serious questions before the reformers as well as the political leaders since the 19th century. It should, however, be noted that except Phule most of the social reformers were concerned with social reforms among the high castes. The problems like widow remarriage and sati were not prevalent among the lower strata of society. And low castes in general irrespective of gender were deprived of education. To the early reformers this division did not present itself very sharply as people like Raja Rammohun Ray articulated women's cause as integral part of his overall vision for what we now referred to as a modern India. Those who began to mobilise opinion regarding the economy and issues related to the operation of the colonial system in the second half of the nineteenth century and early part of the twentieth century were also concerned with the reforms in society and equality of men and a more just society for the women in a possible modern India.

For them the issues of economy and politics were not dissociated. M.G. Ranade, Veereshlingam Pontulu, Gopal Krishna Gokhale, Phirojshah Mehta, Dadabhai Naoroji , Badruddin Tyabji, Jyotiba Phule and many more actively campaigned for women's education and more public space. The symbol of this unity of perception was the fact that the annual conference of the Indian social conference used to meet at the Annual Congress session pandal itself. The question whether the social issue or the political issue is more important emerged by this time. The Congress realised that the differences of perceptions on social issues among different communities were given priority over the political issues, it would breach the unity of people while was essential in the national movement.

In ensuing debate between the social and political question, the idea of priority and the location of the principle of equality was very important. Those who opposed the social conference working anywhere close to the Indian National Congress, in fact, did not oppose the principle of equality. But the separation of the social question from the political turned out to be some way detrimental to the women's questions. The debate on the issue of Age of consent Bill which created an uproar in the 1890s saw that the progressive voices were opposed quite powerfully by sections which were not in favour of a legislation which was primarily a legislation in raising the marriageable age for women. The attempt to separate the two also impeded any serious theoretical debate on the ways and means to incorporate the women's issue in the movement for social equality.

➤ **Women's Issues During the Gandhian Era**

In the 1920s the Gandhian movements brought back a sense of unity on the women's question. Along with the question of untouchability, and Hindu Muslim question, women's condition also became a primary issue to be solved immediately. This has serious implications for the women's movement in general and the mobilisation of women's issues for the larger political context. The national movement now created the largest possible space for the women to come out and participate on an issue which was ostensibly political, i.e., political freedom. But at the same time the masses, including large number of women, were galvanised to raise their own groups' issues in the process of the movement. In 1927 All India Women's Association was formed as the national body giving voice to some of the issues. This was the time when we have voices from women as well as from other sections for giving women the voting rights as well as representation in any possible government formation.

Interestingly, this was also the time that suffrage movement in Europe gained its momentum. Many of the women who were in forefront of the Gandhian movement later became involved in institutions all over the country. These institutions would play a major role in taking up serious social issues, and mobilising and leading movements in later years. In fact, the methods that Gandhi used in his struggle against the colonial state as well as in his movement against the untouchability and on the question of communal conflict became hallmark of some of the movements by women quite often inspired by these women and institutions. In the seventies when women fought in Uttaranchal against the liquor vendors or against the falling of trees, their movement was characterised by the Gandhian ways of protestnon violent and arousing the moral conscience in the opponent.

The success of Russian Revolution in 1970s encouraged a large number of women to join the communist movement in India, who were involved in the national movement and women's movements at the same time. In fact, the communist movement helped the later day progressive movement to take up issues related to women as well as women's position as the central political and social question. These communist women continued their legacy of women's movement in the post-independence period.

THE POST-INDEPENDENCE PERIOD: STATE, REFORM AND WOMEN

The post-independent Indian state launched the array of reforms which had been demanded even before the independence. There were, for example, demands that all customary and religious and traditional laws which regulated the larger Hindu society and which to a great extent therefore determined the legal status of the Hindu women in religious terms should be codified and brought into the public domain. In 1948 there were attempts to bring to the Constituent Assembly what is known as the Hindu code Bill. However, the stiff opposition led to the dropping of the idea. After a couple of other attempts, finally it was in 1955-56 that the Code Bill was passed in sections known as the Hindu Marriage Act, Hindu Succession Act, etc. In spite of the strong support from the Congress party under the leadership of Jawaharlal Nehru the opposition was very strong. The government could not enter into the issue of the personal laws of the other communities, i.e., Muslim, Christian or Parsees. Crucial aspects of their lives continued to be determined by the personal laws of their religious communities in which man was the supreme arbiter in most of the cases.

The post-independent Indian state geared itself to the consensus that modern developed state and the political democracy would be safeguarded by the economic democracy. Women got franchise – the democratic right and the development would see that she got the economic rights to practise that democracy.Thus a full blown theory of equality, rights and justice was in place.

It was the violence against women in the form of bride burning and rape that galvanised the women's movement led by the feminist groups especially since the 1970s. The campaign against dowry and rape are called the first campaigns of the contemporary Indian feminists movement. The violence against women at the ground level, rape by the landlords, caste oppression etc., made the movement gradually try and incorporate them into the concerns for women.

Thus in sum, one of the most important issues concerning women's equality became part of the real politics of the Indian democracy. By the eighties the political movements by communal parties which had a large middle and lower class support gradually affected the original discourse on women and her legal and political entitlements.

THE LEFT AND WOMEN'S MOVEMENTS   Book Q.2

The communist parties, since 1950s, not only provided women leadership but also kept the women's question in the centre of political discussion. However, with the split in the communist movements in 1964 and emergence of many new voices within the left movement which questioned old assumptions of the Marxist parties, new ideas and organisational principles to articulate demands of communities and groups began to emerge. The Shahada movement, in Dhulia district of Maharastra was one such movement.

The exploitation of the local Bhil tribal landless labourers by the non-tribal local landowners was the key issue in this. To add to the woes of the tribals came the successive drought and famine in Maharastra. Different exploitative practices of the landowners and the moneylenders pushed the tribals to take extreme steps of protest. Though the movement had its origin in the late sixties through the traditional folk ways, singing bhajans etc., the seventies saw a complete metamorphosis when the newly inspired left leadership joined the movement and Bhil women were mobilised gradually and in large number. However, in the course of the movement it was realised that the issues that were central to women in these area was not exactly what the organisation had initially thought out as such. For example, after the agitation began in Shahada movement that it was realised that most of the women were landless wage earners and the demand for higher wages would address the women's issue more directly.

In the 1970 again, the Maharastra agitation soon spread to Gujarat where the women in major cities like Bombay, Poona and Ahmedabad came out in streets protesting against the government for such a situation. It happened in the background of economic worsening conditions of the people following Bangladesh War. In Bombay, for example, Socialist Mrinal Gore and Communist Ahilya Rangnekar led the movement. The

Maharastra and Gujarat agitation gradually added to the larger oppositional politics that was being galvanised around this time. In fact, in Gujarat and Maharastra, the lower classes were conspicuous by their absence.

The arrival of the new classes into the picture meant that the political landscape would have become more complex and sharper questions to resolve. Gandhian ideas of femininity and role of female were now questioned and so were the symbols used by him. It is in such a situation that the mobilisation of the women too began to take place. The year 1975 was declared as the world women's year by the United Nations. The Women's decade, 1975-85, witnessed women related activism by feminist groups as well as political parties. These were primarily urban–based activist groups. It was however the state which was promoter of many progressive steps for ameliorating women's condition and saw a large number of activities. Maharastra was hotbed of the left inspired women's activism. The Maoist inspired women organised the Purogami Stree Sangathana (Progressive Women's Association), and Stri Mukti Sangathan in Bombay.

It was also during this time that dalit movement and the feminism got linked. A Mahila Samata Sainik Dal too was formed by some dalit groups in Maharastra. The Maoist groups and the dalit organisations gradually provide a new edge to the argument that religion and caste system provide additional legitimacy to the oppression of women and hence have to be attacked for any possible women's liberation.

EQUALITY OR DIFFERENCE

While the entire edifice of the social movement in India, which wanted to change the status of women, has been raised on the principle of equality, by the eighties there were realisation that even equality was not enough to protect women from being victims of violence perpetrated on her solely because she happened to be a woman. This was in spite of the fact that in many cases she was equal or superior to the male perpetrator in status, education or other indicators. Women were the target of rape simply because she was women – biologically different from Man. It soon became a major theoretical as well as organisational point of debate as to where should the movements place their focus, i.e, on equality or difference. The case of the rape of a tribal girl Mathura in 1987 by the police and despite a campaign and fought by many prominent legal personalities, the judiciary was unmoved and declared Mathura a women of easy virtue. This created uproar and made the women's group realise the insensitivity that the state apparatus has on women's issues. Similarly, the dowry deaths primarily among the affluent middle class households too was a shattering blow to some of the earlier held assumptions, i.e., the development process by raising the status of the women would help her practice her democratic rights fully. The same development was now seen to be capable of making life unsafe for her. By the time the census of 2001 was published, the increasing decline in the sex ratio in the most developed states of India pointed to the same phenomenon.

It was also realised that while it has been pursuing the developmental agenda ostensibly for the betterment of women, the state at times was amenable to the forces of patriarchy. This had further implications. Thus, the feminists and women activists have come to accept that movement for democratisation has to be strengthened so as to strengthen the force behind the demand for better and safer daily lives of women. The need for a strong women's movement got further underlined in the age of globalisation where new forces of violence were unleashed on women.

Issues of not only women's right in a democratic system but also the question of overall equality in a situation when the state is withdrawing is not merely a crucial political issues that the women's movement has to solve.

NEW SOCIAL MOVEMENTS

By the late eighties the overall scenario in India and the world created situation where the women's movement could not remain outside the domain of the issues that have led to the world wide movement regarding ecology, environment and issues of sustainability in the face of the a new globalising economy. Very soon we have movements in different parts of the country, which have voiced the concerns of the day-to-day life and survival in the face of the new forces of economy and politics. While the national politics seems to retreat into the caste and community and costly and corrupt electoral practices, a large number of movements from different parts of the country saw the coming of people from the local communities and villages. One of the chief characteristics of these movements has been the prominent role including that of the leadership being played by women.

Survival and dignity seems to have become the twin issues, which these movements have infused to the already existing issues of equality and justice. Participation of a large number of women in the movement for the rights of labour and the tribals in Chhattisgarh by the Chhattisgarh Mukti Morcha, in the Narmada Bachao Andolan and the agitation against the authorities in Bhanwari Devi case where the authorities were trying the shield the oppressors, and recently in the agitation for rights to information has shown that the social movements have been trying to fuse the issues of politics and society at a larger canvass and convert them into struggles for a more democratic and just society.

Interestingly enough, a careful perusal of the voices from these movements would show that women in these movements have often questioned the validity of the representative nature of our democracy. While they have tried to forge alliances with similar movements across the country and even the world, they have, at the same time, demanded from the state to change its electoral system to have more participation from the women. All these were taking place quite close to the time when a large number of new forces were getting unleashed on the ground without adequately preparing the population for it. The women, without the adequate even elementary education and primary health care facilities, had to face these forces. There were also indications that the state, which till now declared that it would take care of the vulnerable sections, has began to waver and withdraw.

The Women's movement in the meantime also tried to fight against the structures of community and tradition as they have been found quite often to be impediments in the way to equality and freedom. This was evident in the case of two powerful movements in the 1980s, one against the issue of dowry and another in the famous case of Roop Kunwar in which the latter was being burnt as Sati. In cases of the dowry deaths tradition has been forwarded where as in the latter case a young Rajput lady was made to die along with her husband. The opposition by feminist and other groups of the Sati and its later glorification was countered by the powerful combination of the caste and community politics which defended not only the act of sati but also those who forced Roop Kunwar to the funeral pyre. However, in the process there were awareness of the new forces both which supported the women's cause of equality and those opposed came face to face and was an educating for the Women's movement.

10.2: IGNOU Book Exercise – Solved

1) Write a note on the issues of women in the pre-independence period.
Answer by India Ebook: Read the 1 Shot Concept Above.
2) Explain with some examples the mobilisation of women by the leftist forces.
Answer by India Ebook: Read the 1 Shot Concept Above.
3) Explain the role of state regarding women's issues.
Answer by India Ebook: Read the 1 Shot Concept Above.

10.3: IGNOU Past 6 Attempts Question - Solved

Dec 2020(Feb21): Assess the outreach and problems of Women's Movement.
Answer by India Ebook: Refer Introduction above.

NOTES

Introduction

Regional Movement: Meaning and Significance

Methodological Insights on Regional Movements

Regional Movements, Regionalism and State Formation: Some Causative Explanation

Salient Patterns of Movements for Statehood

Types of Regionalism

State's Response to Regional Movements

11.1: One Shot Concepts

INTRODUCTION

As India consists of a large number of regions with diverse social and cultural compositions and different levels development of economy and infrastructure it has been facing regional movements since it became independent. The **Reorganisation** of the **states** in India in **1956** did not solve problems related to regional disparities. Even after the formation of a particular state, a region or more within a state start regional movements for autonomy, independence or even secession from the union of India.

REGIONAL MOVEMENT: MEANING & SIGNIFICANCE Book Q.1

Regional movement is an identity movement seeking special privileges, protection, and concessions from the state. It is a movement for regional self-governance. In other words, it means a movement for state formation — a movement seeking pluralisation and federalisation of existing polity and political process. There are two potential and significant causes of the emergence of regional movement — one is the interregional or intercommunity conflict, and other is the conflict between region and the state.

This is very much evident from recent conflict between Karnataka and Tamilnadu over sharing of Cauvery water, or boarder dispute between Maharashtra and Karnataka, or the most recent conflict between Biharis and Assamese over the competitive examination for central services, or the 'Mumbaikar' call of the Shiv Sena restricting and preventing non-Marathis from occupying important positions in the business, economy and polity of Maharashtra. It is probably the reason that some scholars consider regional movement as consequence of developmental tension between society and polity.

On the other hand, region-state conflict usually takes place in the institutional structure of state system, wherein a region questions the distributive policy of the state as discriminatory, exploitative and unfavourable to the overall well-being of the concerned regional community. It is from this perceived sense of deprivation, neglect and 'internal colonialism' that the people of a particular region organise themselves into a movement seeking in most of the cases separation from the existing state, or in select instances settling with some autonomy arrangements within the same state.

We can now possibly define regional movement as a movement for autonomy of identity and autonomy of development. Its objectives may be accommodative, protectionist, welfarist, autonomist, separatist and secessionist. Secessionism, however, seems to be merely a tactical strategy to pressurise the government. Once their genuine grievances are redressed they settle down within the constitutionally propounded democratic structure of Indian nationalism. There are numerous examples to support this submission, ranging from Tamil separatism to Akali movement (read religious nationalism of Sikhs), Gorkhaland movement, Bodoland movement, etc. A close scrutiny of their demands would suggest that they seek a redefinition of state-society relationship in such a manner that accommodates their identity demands and takes due care of their socio-economic requirement. And to serve this purpose, they usually aspire for a constitutionally documented institutional space of their own where their choices are self-determined. Thus, it is the 'protectionist self' around which politics of regional movement revolves.

METHODOLOGICAL INSIGHTS ON REGIONAL MOVEMENTS

Book Q. 2

Regional movements, especially in a diverse society like India, have contexualised formations. Therefore, it requires a componential analysis of the complex interplay of region, people and the state. When we say regional movement, it immediately refers to the existence of a regional community with political overtone. In more than one sense regional community is different from other social communities. In fact, region may consist of many social communities, which through a highly complex process of nation formation constitute themselves into a distinct regional community.

Componential analysis also helps us in analysing the success, failure and sustenance of a regional movement. It further helps us in examining the nature and potential impact of regional movement on the process of federal nation–building. It is commonly held that more subjectively the identity is grounded, more intense is the regional movement. It is in this context that the theories of nationalism or nation and nationality formation assume critical significance in understanding the phenomena of regional identity formation and its transformation into a movement. Here, it is also worthwhile to consider the similarity and difference between nationalism and regionalism. Regionalism and nationalism are symbiotically linked. Both undergo similar process of construction and formation. They tend to serve their respective social constituencies as an ideology. They share similar analytical concern as to how identity is formed, and when an identity becomes politically salient. Only difference between them is while the nationalism is generally centralising; regionalism, on the contrary, is inherently decentralising. It is possibly the reason that regional movement also emerges as a reaction to nationalism.

In the literatures on nationalism, we find two principally important, but dichotomous accounts of nation-formation: perennialist primordialist; and, modernist. Primordialist considers identity as pre-given entity of distinct races, ethnicity, language, culture, religion etc. These individual attributes of identity are called the objective markers of identity. Any one or combination of them constitutes a distinct national or sub-national community, which when politicised become a distinct nation. Thus for them, nation is a politicised ethno-cultural community, extended in history and deeply rooted in sociocultural traditions.

In India, culture, language, religion, ethnicity, social traditions have assumed regional characteristics. It is probably the reason that we find performative variation in the observance of religious practices and caste idioms from region to region. Another interesting fact about the regions in India is that most of them had some form of administrative identity in the past when people and territory structurally - institutionally enmeshed with each other to give region a particular cultural trait and easily recognisable patterned behavior of the people.

There are **two crucial** submissions of this theory: **(i)** conversion of community into a movement is a process of mobilisation by elite, intellengstia and leaders; and **(ii)** in order to provide further dynamics and cohesion to community consciousness, identity is reinvented and relocated in the contextual present.

From the above discussion, we may now select some crucial variables, which may help us in analysing regional identity and regional movements in India. One of them is federalism. Its working in India has shown some inherent contradiction. As we know, federalism is essentially decentralising. It is a political programme of institutionalising autonomy of society and polity. It is expected to accommodate regionalism within the framework of a federal nationalism. Another important variable is the party system and party structure. The key question to be examined is the coalitional and accommodative capacity of the party system. The hypothesis that can be put forth here is that less coalitional a national party and party system, more intense is the possibility of regional parties to be formed and movement to be organised.

REGIONAL MOVEMENTS, REGIONALISM AND STATE FORMATION: SOME CAUSATIVE EXPLANATION

India has been territorially reorganised into **28 states** and **8 union territories**. Out of this, we have today as many as ~~31~~ **30 demands** for statehood and sub–autonomy arrangements.

They are:

- Maru Pradesh in *Rajasthan*;
- Bundelkhand, Poorvanchal, Bhojpur and Harit Pradesh or Jatland in the *Uttar Pradesh*;
- Vindhya Pradesh, Baghelkhand, Rewanchal, Madhya Bharat, Mahakosal, Malwa in *Madhya Pradesh*;
- Mithila in *Bihar*;
- Saurashtra in *Gujarat*;
- Konkan, Vidarbha and Marathwada in *Maharashtra*;

- ~~Telengana in *Andhra Pradesh*;~~
- Coorg, Kodagu and Sagari Prant in *Karnataka*;
- Kosal Rajya in *Orissa*;
- Gorkhaland and Kamtapuri in *West Bengal*;
- Autonomy demands of *Jammu and Ladakh* regions in Jammu and Kashmir;
- Bodoland, Karbi-Anglong, and Poorbanchal in *Assam*;
- Kukiland in *Nagaland*;
- Garoland in *Meghalaya*; and
- Hmar state in *Mizoram*.

Movements for these states are in different stages of mobilisation. Some of them are strong and persistent, others are dormant but occasionally reiterative.

From close analysis of the official practice of state formation it appears that these demands exist because of the non-congruence between cultural boundary and administrative boundary. In many cases, the present states appear to be invented ones, which has unsuccessfully attempted to create common linguistic, administrative andmpolitical identity among the people living within the different regions of the state.

In the six major and large states of Bihar, Uttar Pradesh, Madhya Pradesh, Rajasthan, Maharashtra and Andhra Pradesh, there alone exist 16 major demands for statehood. Further, in three officially designated Hindi-states of Bihar, Uttar Prdesh and Madhya Pradesh there are as many as eleven demands or movements for separate statehood. The very existence of these demands itself questions the legitimacy of these states being Hindi-States, and their artificial constructedness, In other words, region and state are non-congruent.

On the other hand, in the composite — plural states such as West Bengal, Bihar, Uttar Pradesh, Rajasthan, Gujarat, Maharashtra, Andhra Pradesh and Karnataka, the similar congruence of affinity and interests lacks between the state and people of different regions. Coalescing together many distinct and mutually varying sub-regional identitiesn within one dominant language like Hindi, Bengali, Rajasthani, Gujarati, Marathi, Telegu and Kannada have formed these states. It was believed that these languages would, in due course of time, succeed in creating a broad regional-state identity across the people and sub-regions of these states.

SALIENT PATTERNS OF MOVEMENTS FOR STATEHOOD

The following **salient patterns** of *regional movements* seeking separate state may be discerned:

i) In India, territory and community are symbiotically linked. A region is known by the community, which lives in it, and community is designated and characterised by the geo-specifics of the given region. The demand for separate statehood arises from the synthesis between the two – community and geography. A territorial community seeks separate state in order to be the sole arbiter of its cultural setting, political making and economic wellbeing of the people and territory, which it claims as 'homeland'. For them the state formation means creating an institutionalpolitical space through which 'autonomous self' of the society is not only expressed, but preserved, protected and promoted.

ii) People having distinct socio-cultural identity, concentrated in few contiguous districts within the existing state-systems seek a separate state in order to preserve, protect and promote their identity. It is argued that a separate state would provide them a political identity and a constitutionally documented institutional space for interest articulation and protection within the Indian nation. It is being contested that this would enhance their capacity to bargain with the central authority (union government) as well as with other states in the overall distribution of political power and economic resources.

iii) Some of the above mentioned regional movements seek constitutional recognition, protection and legitimisation of their respective socio-cultural varieties by the state. It is at this level that the demand for functional elevation of mother tongue to the level of education and administration is made. This also includes inclusion of some languages in the eighth schedule of the Constitution of India. Linguistic purism is another facet of socio-cultural regionalism. This in other words means preservation of cultural identity.

iv) Located within the realms of identity and development, regionalism for sub-regional groups serves as an ideology through which they seek to define their own administrative and political identity; and, their relationships with broader territorial state, regional state, and inter-community relationships. Regionalism provides them a bargaining space in the overall process of nationalism and federalism. It acts as countervailing force to centralisation, and allows polity and society to federal. It stresses for a decentralist framework of national unity, nation and state–building, and governance.

TYPES OF REGIONALISM

Iqbal Narain has identified three major types of regionalism (or regional movements) in India (i) **Supra–State** regionalism; (ii) **Inter-State** regionalism; (iii) **Intra-State** regionalism.

Supra–state regionalism is built around the issues of common interest in which group of states form a common political alliance, directed against either the similar alliance of other states or the Union.

Inter-state regionalism, as he further observes, "is coterminous with state boundaries and involves juxtaposing of one or more state identities against another on specific issues, which threaten their interest. River water in general and…boarder dispute in particular can be cited as example.

A regional community against the state in which they are situated spearheads *intra–state* regionalism. Intra–state regionalism is aimed at assuring oneself of self-identity and self-development. This 'self' gradually becomes weak when we move onto other two forms of regionalism. In the case of intra–state regionalism, it is identity around which group's political and economic interests are defined. But in other two cases, it is conflict of interests either between two states or between the centre and the state which temporarily give the people a sense of togetherness, and a common political outlook.

NOTE: Intra means within the State & Inter means One State to Another. (Link with GST…Commerce Background can easily grasp)

STATE'S RESPONSE TO REGIONAL MOVEMENTS   Book Q.4

State's response to regional movements has been varying. We do not find any consistent policy in this regard. However, certain patterns and principles can be discerned in this regard. They are:

(i) secessionist demand could not be conceded, rather, secessionism would be suppressed by all necessary means;

(ii) central government would not concede those regional demands based exclusively upon religious differences; and

(iii) the demands for the creation of separate linguistic would not be conceded unless such a demand is socially wide and economically viable.

To illustrate, there could not be any singular construct or formation of the units of Indian federation. Units should be composite ones. Such a composite unit could be formed only by mutual balancing of four principles which the States Reorganisation Commission (SRC) underlined as:

(i) preservation and strengthening of the unity and security of India;

(ii) linguistic and cultural homogeneity;

(iii) financial, economic and administrative considerations; and

(iv) successful working of the national plan." Other factors like 'peoples' wishes', 'historicity of the region', and 'geographical contiguity' could have only limited, but qualificatory application while (re) drawing the boundary of the units of the Indian Union.

On the basis of SRC's recommendation, the Government of India passed in **November 1956**, the ***State Reorganisation Act***. The Act endorsed the bulk of the recommendations of SRC, except the merger of Hyderabad state into Andhra Pradesh, and Vidarbha was made part of the Bombay state. Thus, the number of **states** was reduced from 16 to **14** in this Act. However, the number of **centrally administered territories** was enhanced from 3 to **6**. The major inclusion was the Himachal Pradesh and Tripura. Since then the numbers of states have been increased to 28 and union territories to 8.

States formed since 1956 include:

Gujarat (1960)	Nagaland (1963)
Haryana (1966)	Punjab (1966)
Himachal Pradesh (1971)	Manipur (1972)
Meghalaya (1972)	Tripura (1972)
Sikkim (1975)	Arunachal Pradesh (1987)
Mizoram (1987)	Goa (1987)
Jharkhand (2000)	Uttaranchal (2000)
Chattisgarh (2000)	Telangana (2014)

Jammu & Kashmir (2019)   Ladakh (2019

11.2: IGNOU Book Exercise – Solved

1) Explain the meaning and significance of regional movements.
Answer by India Ebook: Read the 1 Shot Concept Above.

2) Discuss the methodology to study regional movements.
Answer by India Ebook: Read the 1 Shot Concept Above.

3) Explain the reasons for the rise and growth of regional movements in India.
Answer by India Ebook: Read the 1 Shot Concept Above.

4) Write a note on the response of the state to the regional movements.
Answer by India Ebook: Read the 1 Shot Concept Above.

11.3: IGNOU Past 6 Attempts Question – Solved

Dec 2018: Write notes in about 200 words on each of the following: (a) Regional Movement

Dec 2021: Write short notes in about 200 words each on the following: (a) Regionalism

Answer by India Ebook: Same as **Q.1** Above.

NOTES

12. RELIGIOUS AND COMMUNAL MOVEMENTS

Introduction

What is Communal?

Communal and Religious Movements in Retrospect

Religious Demography

Hindu Communal and Religious Movements

> ➤ Hinduisation and Pedagogic Inculcations
> ➤ Rise of the VHP and the Issue of Conversion
> ➤ Babri Masjid-Ram Janm Bhumi Issue

Islamic Religious and Communal Movements

> ➤ Religio-lingual Issues
> ➤ Communal and Terrorist Activities and Use of Islam

Christian Religious and Social Movements

Sikh Religion and Communal Movements

12.1: One Shot Concepts

INTRODUCTION

Religious and communal movements have been the glaring feature of Indian sub-continent in general and India in particular. Whether it is an issue of social reforms, issue of national awakening, formation of a state or coming to power, the religion has played a decisive role in shaping the destiny of this country and its people. Social movements of varied nature have played an important role in different spheres of life, primarily relating to religion. In South Asia in general and India in Particular, the religious fundamentalist movements have been pivotal in bringing about the socio-political change.

Their influence could be inferred from the fact that even they have been successful in drawing the boundaries of nation state and are constant in such efforts by leading secessionist moments. In addition to this, many of them are quite radical since they even demand a structural change in the system itself from a secular state to a state based on a particular religion. Consequently, such movements indulge in promoting enmity, hostility and violence amongst people of different religions, which raises the question about their legitimacy in the public domain. But in reality, the extent of penetration within the society and linkages with state politics these movements can not be simply dismissed, particularly in the present day India.

WHAT IS COMMUNAL? Book Q.1

In both political parlance and academic discussion, the 'communal' is used in a derogatory sense representing narrow sectarian interests. In pre-independence India, political leaders described the Indian Muslim League a communal organisation. However, for many Marxist and European scholars it represented Muslim nationalism. And in 1946 overwhelming majority of Indian Muslims voted for the Muslim Home Land in the belief that the creation of Pakistan would fulfil Muslim nationalist aspirations in the sub-continent.

Here it is worth pointing out that Communal identities can be formed on territorial, cultural, ethnic, or religious bases or on a combination of these all too, depending upon the emotional intensity that the people attach to a particular aspect of a nation. Both Hindus and Muslims have been mobilised on communal lines. India is not only their Motherland, it is also their sacred land.

In order to achieve geographical unity, places of pilgrimage located in the four corners of the country are often cited and refuge is sought in creating common cultural and religious bonds among the Hindus despite their regional and linguistic differences.

Hindu nationalists emphasise this common cultural and religious bond creating an emotional attachment to this land and its people. The anti-Sikh riots following Indira Gandhi's assassination, the Bhagalpur massacres in 1989, the demolition of the Babri Masjid on December 6, 1992, attacks on missionaries in late nineties and the havoc caused due to the communal riots after the incidence of Godra in 2002 are some of the manifestations of majoritarian communal movements organised on religious lines.

COMMUNAL AND RELIGIOUS MOVEMENTS IN RETROSPECT

The *seeds* of **communalism on religious lines** were sown in the early **British period**. The '**divide and rule policy**' followed by the British Government was largely responsible for the communal hatred amongst the different communities in India.

In the census they categorised people according to religion and viewed and treated them as different from each other. They tried to decipher the Indian communities on the knowledge of basic religious texts and they found intrinsic differences in them instead of the way they coexisted in the present. The British remained fearful of the potential threat from the Muslims, who were the former rulers of the subcontinent, ruling India for over 300 years under the Mughal Empire. In order to win them over to their side, the British helped establish the M.A.O. College at Aligarh and supported the All-India Muslim Conference, both of which became the forerunner institutions from which leaders of the Muslim League and the ideology of Pakistan emerged.

The social reformer and educator, **Sir Syed Ahmed Khan**, who <u>founded</u> **M.A.O. College**, taught the Muslims that education and cooperation with the British was vital for their survival in the society. Tied to all the movements of Muslim revival was the opposition to assimilation and submergence in Hindu society. Sir Syed Ahmed Khan was also the first to conceive of a separate Muslim homeland. The idea of the separateness of Muslims in India was built into the electoral process of India following the introduction of separate electorate which culminated in ideological schism between the Muslims and the Hindus in time to come. While there were strong feelings of nationalism in India against the British, by the late 19th century there were also communal conflicts and movements in the country that were based on religious communities rather than class or region.

Along with Muslim communalism, **Hindu communal sentiments** were also fanned on the issues of 'cow slaughter', conversion by Christians and Muslims. Shuddhi Movement was launched to reconvert the Hindus, who embraced Islam or Christianity, by the Hindu revivalists like Arya Samaj and other Hindu orthodox organisations.

In response to the formation of **Muslim League**, *Hindu Right Wing* political movements also started getting organised on political lines in full swing in the form of **Hindu Mahasabha** and Rashtriya Swayamsevak Sangh (**RSS**) in the beginning quarter of twentieth century, claiming for a unified <u>**Hindu-Rashtra.**</u>

The political ideology, formed on the religious sentiments, could not keep together the communities living in this sub-continent, despite strong secular nationalist sentiments reflected during the freedom struggle. The independence of India accompanied its partition on communal lines, though India altogether discarded the formation of state on religious or communal sentiments and declared itself a secular state. However, as the religious values and sentiments were integral to Indian society at large, they kept on echoing the hearts of masses in one or the other issues raised on religious lines.

Despite, having accepted the partition on communal lines the majority-minority syndromes remained intact. Numbers of Muslims inhabiting India are the same as in Pakistan making it one of the largest Muslim countries of the world. To further understand the gravity of the situation on account of its religious multiplicity where communal movements are still able to disturb the social harmony, it would be desirable to have an insight into the demographic composition as pointed out by the census of 2001.

RELIGIOUS DEMOGRAPHY

The country has a total area of approximately 1.3 million square miles and a population of slightly more than one billion. According to the latest government estimates, Hindus constitute 82 per cent of the population, Muslims 12 per cent, Christians 2.3 per cent, Sikhs 2.0 percent, and others, including Buddhists, Jains, Parsis (Zoroastrians), Jews and Baha'is, less than 2 per cent. It is difficult to define Hinduism as Hindus worship many Gods and Goddesses, and rituals also vary from region to region and caste to caste. Slightly more than 90 per cent of Muslims are Sunni; the rest are Shia. Buddhists include followers of the Mahayana and Hinayana schools and there are both Catholic and Protestant Christians.

Tribal groups (members of indigenous groups historically outside the caste system), which in government statistics generally are included among Hindus, often practice traditional indigenous religions. Hindus and Muslims are spread throughout the country, although large Muslim populations are found in the states of Uttar Pradesh, Bihar, Maharashtra, West Bengal, Andhra Pradesh, and Kerala, and Muslims are a majority in

Jammu and Kashmir. Christian concentrations are found in the North-Eastern states, as well as in the southern states of Kerala, Tamil Nadu, and Goa. Three small North-Eastern states have large Christian majorities—Nagaland, Mizoram, and Meghalaya. Sikhs are a majority in the state of Punjab. In the last half century or so, many lower caste Hindus, Dalits (called as 'Scheduled Castes') and other non-Hindu tribal groups have converted to other faiths because they viewed conversion as a means to escape widespread discrimination and achieve higher social status.

With such a vast and diverse religious configuration and having the history of rich religious origins, it is but natural that people of this land are bound to get influenced in their public or private activities by religious sentiments. In order to assert their religious identity in social and political life, all the communities have tried to woo the masses by raising emotive issues more often resulting in destructive tendencies, affecting the nation building process and causing embitterment in the social harmony.

HINDU COMMUNAL AND RELIGIOUS MOVEMENTS   Book Q.3

Hindu revivalists movements during the 19th century prepared the ground for right wing politics along which religious issues took the shape of Hindu communalism. The issues of conversion, ban on cow slaughter, implementation of Hindi, Hinduisation of education and asserting the claim of Hindu homeland remained vibrant even after independence. Adding further to the communal frenzy, the issues like, Uniform Civil Code, **removal of Article 370** (related to Kashmir), demolition of Babri Masjid (a historical mosque) and construction of Ram Temple on the same place and subsequent attacks on Christian missionaries on account of their policy of proselytisation, remained the bone of contention on which Hindu right wing social movements thrived and tried to enchant the masses.

The issues based on identities of religion, caste and ethnicity have overshadowed the social and political processes after independence. The diversity on ascriptive denominations, on which the religious communal movements were based, attempted social transformation whereby a homogeneous polity could be established or at least, the dominance of the majority community be asserted and other religious groups are reduced to just the status of foreigners.

The Hindu Mahasabha, which was the major political force before independence and which spoke for the cause of Hindus, diminished because of Mahatma Gandhi's assassination and umbrella like domination of Indian National Congress. After independence the other Hindu outfits were also put to the test of time and got little recognition in independent India because of the ugly face of communal violence which killed millions and displaced around 15 Million people across the border. The brutal assassination of Mahatma was the single event at the time of Independence which made people indifferent towards religious sentiments in the public life.

However, the RSS continued to penetrate the masses through its social service projects and resuscitated the Hindu national spirit through a large network of tens and thousands of shakhas, engaged in its multifarious Seva projects undertaken by its various suborganisations in the field of student, labour, farming, education and in especially Vanavasi areas.

> ### Hinduisation of Pedagogic Inculcations

The socio-economic and cultural reforms, which the RSS undertook after independence, were extensive and got a wide ranging recognition amongst the Indian masses. The RSS, in order to achieve its objectives, stroked at the roots of mass inertia. It sought to alter the social formation through pedagogic programmes, voluntary social work during natural calamities and repeated assertion for the Hindu-Rashtra for Hindus.

In line with other social reformist movements like the Arya Samaj or the Ramakrishna Mission, the RSS started its agenda of penetration through wide ranging educational institutions which inculcated pedagogic programmes on traditional Hindu lines. To this effect, the RSS started the first Saraswati Shishu Mandir in 1952 in Gorakhpur (Uttar Pradesh). As the number of schools grew in different states, an all-India co-ordinating body called Vidya Bharati was set up with its headquarters in Delhi. The Vidya Bharati educational mission was founded with the objective of training children to see themselves as protectors of a Hindu nation.

The RSS practices may be seen as a reaction to the widespread Christian missionary educational practices. In their efforts to revive past culture, Sanskrit terms are used to address teachers (Acharya), the practice of touching their feet as a mark of respect and the naming of classrooms after Hindu sages ('Vashisht kaksh', 'Vishwamitra kaksh'), also marks out the school as a space where Hindu Dharma and Hindu Sanskars are asserted with pride, where tradition is saved and transmitted as against the 'enculturation' or 'influence of Christianity' through convent missionaries.

The RSS/BJP has attempted to affect a radical departure in the existing educational ethos through the use of both state power by packing state educational institutions with its own ideologues and the instruments of 'civil society', where it created its own network of schools in order to feed the well-developed cadre structure of its organisations.

Inevitably, the RSS's educational and political agenda included both: absorbing subaltern groups into the Hindu fold to fight against 'minorities' and using violence against these same groups in order to perpetuate Hindu dominance in the existing social order. In order to justify and make their inculcations logical, the Sangh Parivar took recourse to re-write historical developments which shaped the destiny of India.

➢ Rise of the VHP and the Issue of Conversion

The process of religious conversion has evoked grave concerns amongst the members of the Sangh Parivar down the century which were intensified and made to appear much more legitimate by giving the loss a 'patriotic' and 'national' colour. This phenomenon has been a key to the functioning of Hindu majoritarianism particularly after 1947. The Sangh Parivar's justifications of recent outrages against Christians are in consonance with the instances of such an equation.

It is widely assumed that Hinduism zis unique among religious traditions in being nonproselytising. Conversion to other faiths, therefore, is a loss that cannot be recovered. This logic at once echoes at the hearts of most of the individuals. The common sense, which is applied here, is that one can become a Hindu by birth alone since caste (whether in the Varna or the Jati sense) is crucial to Hinduism and caste status is hereditary.

From the late 19th century onwards as the expansion directed towards marginal groups and tribals became more organised, 'reclamation', Shuddhi (purification), 'reconversion'(Parivartan, 'turning back'—the term preferred by the VHP today) became more rampant. All these terms have been coined to bring people back to their 'natural' state, presuming that all the targeted groups are Hindu in a more or less Sanskritised manner. If we analyse the functioning of the Jana Sangh in early days, along with the promotion of highly Sanskritised Hindi and cow-protection, the fight against Christian missionaries was made an important plank of its activities. The Jan Sangh organised an Anti-Foreign Missionary Week in Madhya Pradesh in November 1954.

In addition to Pokhran blasts and swiftly accelerated 'liberalisation', the BJP-dominated coalition at centre may be remembered for the concerted campaign against Christians. The widespread revulsion evoked by the sheer horror of the Staines' killings on 23 January 1999 seemed to have produced a brief lull but then the attacks started again and came to be more and more widely distributed. By August 2000 they had spread to a very big part of the country: Uttar Pradesh, Haryana, Punjab, Madhya Pradesh, Andhra, Karnataka, Tamilnadu and Goa. A recent Christian estimate places the number of recorded attacks since 1998 at 184, while there have been 35 incidents in the first six months of 2000 alone.

Babri Masjid-Ramjanm Bhoomi Issue

The resurgent spirit of Hindu communal assertion finally found a historic expression in the Ayodhya movement which Shri Girilal Jain described as the most significant event after Independence. The RSS holds the view that Ayodhya, Mathura and Kashi is not a political but a national question.

This issue further aggravated the situation. The events between 1986-92 have an interesting account to present. Though the controversy of Ramjanm Bhoomi has more than a century old history, yet it remained within the four walls of Ayodhya. Even on 28 December 1949 when riots broke out due to the sudden installation of Ram Lalla's idol over-night, the incidence could not gain much heat as the doors of the Mosque were swiftly closed for both the communities and place was kept under guard in status quo till 1985 when Rajeev Gandhi ordered the opening the Gate of controvertial Babri Masjid for Pooja by the Hindus. Adding to this, the Doordarshan serial—Ramayana further acted as a catalyst to this controversy. The Sangh Parivar used the actors of the serial for gaining support in the elections of 1989. The campaign was launched from the district of Faizabad in which the town of Ayodhya was located, symbolising the strong urge for a Hindu assertion.

Even Rajeev Gandhi wanted to capitalise on this issue, though in a subtle manner. He tacitly allowed the foundation stone for the proposed Ram Temple to be laid adjacent to the Mosque. Rajeev Gandhi did not hesitate to refer to this incident being similar to Mahatma Gandhi's dream for Ram Rajya. However, those involved directly with the movement were the real beneficiaries. The VHP was confident that the Babri Mosque controversy would split every party vertically. These gestures of the VHP came true to a greater extent as the BJP's electoral gains were considerable.

Despite its repeated threats after 1992, the VHP and other Hindu outfits have largely refrained from taking direct confrontation with the State. Now they have moderated their agenda, i.e. settling the issue through court, though there have been oscillations of their anger in repeated threats to the state time and again.

In March 2003, the VHP announced it would launch a nationwide campaign to 'reclaim' 30,000 Hindu temples that had been converted into mosques. Some Muslims fear that under this campaign, Hindus will try to claim the Gyan Vapi mosque in Varanasi, the Idgah mosque in Mathura, and the Ram temple grounds at the former Babri Mosque in Ayodhya.

The VHP continued its trident of 'trishul' distribution programme during the reporting period despite the prohibition under the Penal Code against the distribution of sharp weapons to the public. Trishuls (three-pronged tridents) are Hindu religious symbols, but they have also been used as weapons, including in the **2002 Gujarat riots**.

ISLAMIC RELIGIOUS AND COMMUNAL MOVEMENTS

Islam is one of the largest minority faiths in India and is perceived by Sangh Parivar as actively engaging a pan-Islamic ideology in order to recover the past glory, and constantly is the cause of the Hindu sense of insecurity.

Along with Hindu religious and social movements in the 19th century, the rising tide of Muslim politics was quite visible in the first quarter of 20th century particularly after the formation of All India Muslim League in 1906. The Muslim communalism, like other right wing organisations started acquiring colour on religio-political lines and inhibited the integration and assimilation of Muslim community in Indian society. Aligarh Muslim University fuelled the fire by giving communal colour to issues like Urdu language and separate electorates for Muslims and steadily accelerated the movement for communal politics in the name of religious brotherhood. Events like Khilafat Movement, Mopla riot in Kerala, propaganda of two-nation theory, demand for Pakistan and finally the partition of the country were the outcome of such politics fanned on religious lines.

Even after the formation of secular India, the demands for maintaining exclusive identity remained consistent. The concept of religious brotherhood was put to use for this purpose. The cry for 'Islam is in danger' caught the imaginary concept of Muslim brotherhood or the religious solidarity of the Muslims, which formed the main ingredient of Muslim politics in India. Some of the Muslim scholars have rightly pointed out this divisive communal design of the feudal section in the community.

> ### Religio-lingual Issues

Along with the demand for separate electorate, the Urdu Language has also acquired religious colour. Muslims, irrespective of their region and Mother tongue, have constantly raised the issue of Urdu as a part of their religio-cultural heritage.

It is a general perception of the Muslims in India that Urdu can and will survive in India as a functional language only through its inclusion in the educational curriculum as a Modern Indian Language, which is the mother-tongue of more than 60 million Indians. However, due to the negligent attitude of the so called secularists and Hindu right wing ideologues, Urdu is losing its glory. Here, they generally forget that even rich language like Sanskrit could not survive despite having achieved State protection.

No one denies the glare of Urdu as one of the fabulous languages of India but here, people belonging to Islamic faith should not claim for its monopoly over this lingua franca which is even spoken by those who do not subscribe to this faith. The kind of communal colour which associates with this language, Urdu has become largely confined to Muslim minority educational institutions and religious seminaries called Madrasas.

Though it has survived, yet the learners now belong to the lower strata of the Muslim community which is not only economically backward but socially fragmented too, which consequently renders it as one of the educationally backward and deprived communities in the country. Thus, the religious aspect has come to define the horizons of Urdu due to the denial of state support or rather the denial of the constitutional rights of the Urdu-speaking community. It is this situation which has misdirected the postindependence discourse on Urdu. To some extent, the preservation of Urdu is linked to the economic survival of the backward sections of the Muslim community since the Muslim elite of North India has altogether abandoned the language. No doubt Urdu is the repository of the religious heritage of Muslim Indians yet, as a spoken language, it is still lingua franca of common man of India.

> ➤ **Communal and Terrorist Activities and Use of Islam**

Apart from these issues which have largely dominated the mind set of Muslim population of India to a larger extent, the Islamisation of communal violence, separatism and terrorism have too come up as the special feature of religious communalism of Muslims in India, especially in the state of Jammu and Kashmir.

The Government officially banned the Students Islamic Movement of India (SIMI) in September 2001 under the Unlawful Activities Prevention Act for 'fomenting communal tension' and actions 'prejudicial to India's security.' The Government alleged that the SIMI had links with terrorist groups such as the Lashkar-e-Tayyeba and the Hizbul Mujahideen. The police in three different states arrested eight of its members, including former president of the SIMI Bhopal district unit,

Khalid Naeem. On May 3, 2001, likewise government banned the Muslim group Deendar Anjuman for 'fomenting communal tension' and actions 'prejudicial to India's security'. State prosecutors alleged that some members of the tiny Muslim group called Deendar Channabasaveshwara Siddique (DCS) and its parent organisation, Deendar Anjuman, were responsible for the Karnataka and Andhra Pradesh church bombings in 2000. Given the terrorist insurgency throughout the globe, the Islamic groups are the easy target of state in most of the non-Islamic countries.

12.2: IGNOU Book Exercise - Solved

1) What do you understand by the phenomenon of communalism? How far religions have contributed to its growth in India?

Answer by India Ebook: Read the 1 Shot Concept Above.

3) "Majority communalism is more dangerous than minority communalism." Comment.

Answer by India Ebook: Read the 1 Shot Concept Above.

12.3: IGNOU Past 6 Attempts Question - Solved

Dec 2018: Discuss how the Bhakti Movement has contributed to Indian social harmony.

Answer by India Ebook: Refer Concept above.

June 2019: What is communalism? How does it work in India?

Answer by India Ebook: Almost same as **Q.1** above.

June 2020: Write a note on religious movements in India.

Answer by India Ebook: Write all Religious Movements (Hindu, Islam, Sikh & Christian) in Brief.

NOTES

____

____

____

____

____

____

____

13. AGRARIAN MOVEMENTS

Introduction

What are the Agrarian Movements and Agrarian Classes?

> Meaning
> Differentiation within the Agrarian Classes

Approaches to Study Agrarian Movements

Agrarian Movements in the Pre-Independence Period

Agrarian Movements in the Post-Independence Period

> Rural Poor: Agricultural Labourers and Small/Poor/Marginal Peasants
> Farmers/Middle Peasants/Kulaks/Rich Peasants/Rural Rich
> Globalisation and Farmers' Movements

13.1: One Shot Concepts

INTRODUCTION

Different agrarian classes have resorted to collective action through out the pre-Inpendence and post-Independence periods. The volume of participation of the classes, response of the state and success of the agrarian movements have depended on the nature of leadership, issues, patterns of mobilisation and the attitude of the authorities. These days the agrarian movements are referred to as among the social movements. This unit discusses the agrarian movements, the reasons and context of their rise or fall, nature of issues taken up by them, nature of leadership and patterns of mobilisation. The basic focus of the unit is on those agrarian movements which took place in the post-Independence period.

WHAT ARE THE AGRARIAN MOVEMENTS AND AGRARIAN CLASSES?

> **Meaning**   **June 2021**

Agrarian movements include the movements of agrarian classes which are related to agriculture in terms of working on the land or in terms of both working on land and its ownership. In other words, these are the movements of the agricultural labourers, poor and small peasant/ tenants and farmers/kulaks/rich peasants/rural rich. The issues taken up in the agrarian movements are generally economic. But in several cases the economic and social issues overlap. Such cases include where the agrarian class is both an economic and social group; for example in the case of dalits and women the economic and social (self-respect, dignity and gender based discrimination) are also involved.

> ### Differentiation within the Agrarian Classes   Book Q.1

Agrarian society is not a homogeneous unit. It is divided on economic and social basis. The mobilisation of an agrarian group depends on the specific issues related to it. The collaboration between different groups or conflict among them also depends on the convergence of the group interests. Therefore, in order to understand the movements of different agrarian classes it is necessary to discuss the criteria to designate a particular class. There two broad frameworks which are used by the scholars to differentiate or identify different agrarian classes —, i.e., non-Marxian and the Marxian. The advocates of the former take into consideration the multiple factors like caste, geographical zones and size of land holdings to identify the agrarian classes.

i) The Rural Poor: Agricultural labourers and small/poor/marginal peasants — Agricultural labourers do not own land but work on others land for wages either as agricultural labourers or tenants. Small/poor/marginal peasants have land but it not enough to meet the basic needs. They have to work on others land also; and

ii) Farmers/middle peasants/kulaks/rich peasant/rural rich — These classes own land and other required paraphernalia in agriculture. They work on their land or do not work themselves except doing the supervisory work along with employing agricultural labourers.

APPROACHES TO STUDY AGRARIAN MOVEMENTS

Traditionally there have been two approaches to study the agrarian movements – the Marxian and non-Marxian. The former analyse these movements in the light of the social relations of production or the economic relations – how the poorer agrarian classes get mobilised against their exploitation by the exploiting classes. The latter give more emphasis to the cultural and non-economic factors. In the early 1980s there was an addition to the Marxian approach. Influenced by the Gramsci's writings this approach came to be known as the subaltern approach. Subaltern school has had the most profound impact on the study of the agrarian movements. It has been popularised by Ranajit

Guha in the series of subaltern studies. This approach is critical of the classical Marxism, which gives primacy to the economic factors over other factors. The subaltern school argues that the peasants have their own consciousness, leadership and other cultural factors which play much more important role than the class. The sublatern school is also critised by classical Marxists as separating consciousness and culture from the economic structure and thus not giving the true picture of the reality. Rajender Singh analyses the secondary literature on the agrarian movements as parts of the social movements in the post-Marxian perspective in his book Social Movements, Old and New: Post-Modernist Critique.

AGRARIAN MOVEMENTS IN THE PRE-INDEPENDNECE PERIOD

Book Q.2

Ghanshyam Shah while reviewing the literature on social movements in India in the book Social Movements in India: A Review of Literature points out that Political Science has been averse to the peoples' participation in politics and movements. Almost all regions of the country witnessed agrarian movements during the pre-Independence period. Popularly known as the peasant movements, these movements involved all exploited classes – tenants, agricultural labourers, artisans, etc. Ranajit Guha, actually includes those landlords as exploited classes who were indebted to the moneylenders. Among the most prominent of these movements were Oudh peasant movements in UP, Kheda movement in Guajarat, Mopilla movement in Malabar (Kerala), Champaran peasant movement in Bihar, Wahabi, Fairabi and Tebhaga movements of Bengal and Telengana movement in Madras presidencies (areas forming present Andhra Pradesh).

Agrarian movements of these two phases — pre and post-Independence. The pre-Independence period movements can be termed as the anti-colonial movements as well, since these movements were against the classes which were supporters of the British empire — the landlords, moneylenders and other exploiting classes. The issues raised in these movements were related to the nature of agrarian relations. These relations were built on the exploitation of the agrarian classes — tenants/peasants/agricultural labourers, artisans, etc. In order to meet the requirement of the colonial forces and to satisfy their feudal needs, the landlords exploited them in several ways. These included unreasonable increase in the rent, forced gifts (nazarans), begar (forced labour) physical torture, insecurity of tenure (eviction). These problems were compounded by natural calamities like famines and flood, commercialisation of crops, indebtedness. The failure to meet the economic and non-economic requirements of the landlords the poor agrarian classes were not only evicted from the land they cultivated they were also tortured physically.

The leadership of the peasant movements of the pre-Independence period articulated the problems of the peasants and mobilised them into action against the landlords, moneylenders and the British administration. The general point which emerges from a large number of studies is that the leadership of these movements came from the non-peasant classes.

The peasant movements of the pre-Independence period had impact on the programmes of the Indian National Congress. The Congress Socialist group within the Congress which included later generation of socialists, communists and future Prime Minister of India advocated the need for the drastic land reforms. The Congress appointed a committee to look into the distress of agrarian classes and to suggest measures to ameliorate their conditions. This had its impact on the agrarian policies of country when it became independent. As the land reforms became the state subject, depending on the willingness and political will of the leadership, land reforms became the subject to reckon with in different states of India.

AGRARIAN MOVEMENTS IN POST-INDEPENDENCE PERIOD

Certain developments in Indian political economy of the post-Independence era can provide landmarks about the genesis and decline of the agrarian movements. These are the policy measures introduced by the state during the 1950s, both at the national and provincial levels to bring about the agrarian transformation — through land reforms, community development programmes and agricultural Extension schemes; the green revolution in select areas of the country during the 1960s, and opening of agricultural sector to the world market through the latest phase of globalisation from the 1990s.

These developments have resulted in emergence of new set of issues, rise of new agrarian classes and decline of erstwhile classes, new types of organisations and patterns of political mobilisation. This section of the unit discusses movements of different agrarian classes. These classes are agricultural labourers, poor and small peasants and the farmers/middle peasants/kulaks/rich peasants/rural rich.

> ### Rural Poor: Agricultural Labourers and Small/Poor/Marginal Peasants

The rural poor is a conglomerate of the poorer classes — landless agricultural labourers, tenants, poor, small or marginal farmers who own uneconomic landholdings and supplement their income by working as wage labourers either in agriculture or informal non-agrarian sectors. Most them belong to low castes — lower backwards and dalits.

Unlike the kulaks/middle/rich peasants they face dual problems — social discrimination and economic exploitation. Therefore, while the mobilisation of the better off agrarian classes has mainly been around the economic issue, that of the rural poor has focused both on the social and economic issues. They are sometimes mobilised exclusively on the social and cultural issues, they are also mobilised mainly on the economic issues. Assertion of dalit identity, mainly under the influence of Ambedkarism through different social and cultural organisations of dalits, finding expression in different ways including conversion to another religions are examples of mobilisation on the social and cultural issue.

The agricultural labourers and poor/small peasants have been mobilised into collective actions through out the post-Independence era in different states of India by different kinds of organisations. The latter included the socialist and communist parties, Gandhians, voluntary groups/NGOs, independent individuals and naxalites. This sub-section discusses some examples of movements of agrarian classes which form the rural poor.

The first two decades following Impendence saw the movements of the rural poor in Uttar Pradesh by the socialists and communists on the one hand and by the naxalites and the Communist Party of India on the other hand. The issues on which they were mobilised in the western Uttar Pradesh included redistribution of the Gaon Samaj land, abolition of begar, giving better wages, lifting of the sanction imposed by the rich classes on the poorer classes for cutting grass needed as fodder from the fields of the former, and protection of the women of the poorer classes from the exploitation of the men belonging to the richer classes. The forms of protest included hunger strike and

demonstrations. The 1960s also saw the mobilisation of dalits by Republican Party of India, which unlike the BSP of the later period took up the cultural issues along with the economic problems.

> ### Farmers/Middle Peasants/Kulaks/Rich Peasants/Rural Rich
Book Q.3

The two decades of the last century — the sixties and seventies, witnessed the movements of a section, which is known by different names — farmers, middle peasants, kulaks, rich peasants or rural rich. These movements had their own organisations and leadership. These movements were: those of two separate organisations of the same name — the **Bharatiya Kisan Unions** (BKUs) led by Bhupender Singh Mann in Punjab and by Mahender Singh Tikait in Uttar Pradesh; of Shetkari Sangathan led by Sharad Joshi in Maharashtra; of Karnataka Rajya Raitha Sangha led by Prof. Nanjundaswami; of Khedyut Samaj in Guajarat; of Vivasayigal Sangam led by Narayanaswami Naidu in Tamil Nadu.

Characteristics

These movements shared certain characteristics: they emerged in prosperous regions of the country, which have benefited from the green revolution; they were the movements of rural rich, which included rich peasants, landlords and self-cultivating middle peasants in which the middle peasants had the preponderance; these groups had benefited from the land reforms including the abolition of landlordism; socially the middle or intermediate castes (Jats, Gujars, Yadavs, Muslim high castes in UP; Marathas in Maharashtra; Vokaliggas and Lingayats in Karnataka; Patels in Guajrat) formed the largest composition of them); unlike the peasant movements of the pre-Independence period their issues and demands are related to the market economy like remunerative prices of the agricultural produce, subsidised inputs, reduction in the electricity bills, increase in the time of availability of electricity; their "apolitical" or "non-political" character; claim to represent the rural (bharat) interests against urban (India) on the plea the bharat is exploited by India; they overlook the division in the rural society and project themselves to be representative of entire rural society; they were being led by a new kind of leadership; they raise new types of issue, etc.

Of these three movements — Shetkari Sangathan in Maharashtra, Karnataka Raitha Sangha in Karnataka and BKU movement of UP deserve special discussion for different reasons. It was the "Bharat vs. India" thesis of Sharad Joshi which highlighted the ruralurban divide more prominently.

> **Genesis of Farmers' Movements**   Book Q.4

Since farmers movements are the post- green revolution movements and largely occurred in the green revolution belt, they found the terms of trade against the agricultural sector. The rising cost of input in agriculture could not be met with the returns of the produce. Besides, inability of the system to provide electricity along with the increasing indebtedness to the public institution mainly to meet the input and infrastructural requirement gave birth to the new set of problems of the farmers. Though placed in superior position to the large proportion of the rural poor, this section found itself neglected by the state.

Under these circumstances the farmers responded positively to alternative mode mobilisation, which was marked by the mobilisation on the "apolitical" or "nonpolitical" plank, projected the rural sectors as a homogeneous unit, which was exploited by the urban vested interests. The leadership which not was professional type found it easy to provide leadership to these movements. The example of the BKU movement in UP can be an appropriate example in this context. It was the last of these movements; while other farmers movements took place in the 1970s and the early 1980s, the BKU movement of UP took place mainly in 1988-1989. It was a time when there was complete vacuum of leadership of the farmers caused by the death of Charan Singh on May 29, 1987 and earlier disintegration of the farmers movement in UP following the death of R M Lohia in 1967.

➢ Farmers' Movements before the BKU   Book Q.4

Prior to the BKU mobilisation in the 1980s, the farmers of UP were mobilised mainly by the leftist forces which included both the socialists and the communists. But their mobilisation mainly took place in the 1950s and the 1960s. Apart from the socialists and communists, Charan Singh also attempted to mobilise the farmers of UP during this period. But he did not mobilise them into a collective action. He, in fact, was opposed to the agatitions. His mobilisation of farmers was in the form of carving out an electoral base for himself among the middle and backward caste peasants like Jats, Yadavs, Kurmies, Kories, Lodhs, etc of UP. He did so while he was still a member of the Congress. He adopted two-pronged policy for this purpose: first, he articulated the interests of the peasant proprietors; second, he identified himself with the backward caste peasantry.

The principal issue of the mobilisation was related to cane price, though other issues also mattered. Therefore, the peasant movement in UP was basically sugar cane growers' movements. Through out the 1950s and 1960s the sugar cane growers were mobilised by the socialists and communists during the months of December and March - the peak season for sugar cane harvesting under the banners of organisations like Hind Kisan Panchayat and Kisan Sabha. They resorted to organising rallies, dharnas at the mill gates, conferences of the peasants, etc.

➢ Globalisation and Farmers' Movements   Book Q.5

Unlike the earlier movements those of the farmers in the era of globalisation have reacted to the issues related to globalisation. The attempt of the western countries, especially to interfere in the agrarian economy of the country, especially through the Dunkel Draft and GATT evoked different reactions from the farmers movement. While Sharad Joshi, the Shetkari Sangathan leader from Maharashtra supported the globalisation, two supported leaders Prof. Nanjudaswami of Karntaka Rajya Rytha Sangha and Mahendra Singh Tikait of BKU in UP opposed it. Sharad Joshi argued that the opening of Indian agriculture to the world competition would benefit Indian farmers. His perspective helped him to become an advisor to the Government of India during the regime of V. P. Singh. The opponents of globalisation Nanjudaswami and Tikait got support of academic activist like Vandana Shiva and a large number of the socialist and Gandhians. They argued that that globalisation would not only expose the Indian farmers to the unequal competition with the European farmers, an attempt to change the patent laws about seeds would deprive them of their traditional rights over the preservation and generation of seeds. They opposed the attempt of the government to change the patent laws, demanded abrogation of the subsidies given by the European governments to their

farmers. They also opposed the Multinational Companies which used Indian natural resources like water to manufacture soft drinks. In fact, intellectuals like Vandana Shiva argue that modern technology popularised in green revolution has harmed the fertility of land rather than helping it. The opponents of the globalisation organise rallies, demonstration and seminars to register their protest. Following the death of Prof. Nanjudaswami the farmers protest against globalisation has got weakened.

13.2: IGNOU Book Exercise – Solved

1) How can you differentiate within the agrarian society?
Answer by India Ebook: Read the 1 Shot Concept Above.

2) Write a note on the peasant movements in the pre-Independence period.
Answer by India Ebook: Read the 1 Shot Concept Above.

3) Compare the characteristics of movments of the rural poor with those of the rich peasants.
Answer by India Ebook: Read the 1 Shot Concept Above.

4) Write a note on the farmers movements of the post-Independence period.
Answer by India Ebook: Read the 1 Shot Concept Above.

5) How did the farmers movements react to the globalisation? Discuss.
Answer by India Ebook: Read the 1 Shot Concept Above.

13.3: IGNOU Past 6 Attempts Question – Solved

June 2021: Write notes: (b) Agrarian movement in India.
Answer by India Ebook: Refer **Meaning** above as marked.

June 2020, Dec 2018: Write notes: (b) State and Farmers Movement
Answer by India Ebook: Almost same as **Q.4** above.

Introduction
What is Working Class Movement?
Development of Capitalist Enterprises
Workers' Movements before the Emergence of Trade Unions
Emergence and Growth of Trade Unions
  - ➢ The Beginning
  - ➢ Formation of the AITUC and Subsequent Developments
  - ➢ Division and Political Affiliation
The Movement in the Post-Independence Period

14.1: One Shot Concepts

INTRODUCTION

The modern working class arose in India in the nineteenth century. This development was due to the establishment of modern factories, railways, dockyards and construction activities relating to roads and buildings. It was a modern working class in the sense of relatively modern organisation of labour and a relatively free market for labour. There were certain important exceptions to this rule. The plantation workers, who also worked for the capitalist employers and produced goods which were sold in the international markets, were recruited and worked under unfree conditions. In fact, for the majority of the workers in colonial India, the recruitment and working conditions were not as free as were present in some other countries which were capitalistically more developed. This situation had its impact on the working class movement as it developed over the years. Apart from less developed economy, the colonial condition also had its bearing on the labour movement.

WHAT IS WORKING CLASS MOVEMENT?   Book Q.1

It must be clarified right in the beginning that working class movement and trade union movement are not exactly the same thing. They are different in the sense that the **working class movement** is a much *broader phenomenon* and *covers all kinds of movements* involving workers. It includes within its ambit silent protests, passive resistance, individual protests and strikes as well as more organised forms of welfare activities and bigger protests and strikes reaching to the level of general strikes. It involves various kinds of reactions and responses of the workers to the industrial system.

These reactions may be to ameliorate the working and living conditions within the industrial system, but they may also be radically opposed to the industrial system itself. Thus labour movement may range from everyday struggles of the workers to general strikes encompassing the whole industry or many industries. It covers the activities and movements of the workers within the capitalist system as well as those opposed to it.

Trade union movement, on the other hand, accepts the industrial system as given but attempts to make it more humane, more amenable to the needs of the workers. It tries to reform the working and living conditions of the workers within the industrial system. The short-term and long-term working of the trade unions is geared towards making the workers more committed to the industrial work while agitating for higher wages, suitable working conditions, stable housing and reasonable credit system. While labour movement may include various types of structures, pre-industrial or modern in nature, which coordinate the protest activities of the workers, the trade unions are generally hierarchical and bureaucratic, relying upon a variety of functionaries with defined roles. The trade unions run on the basis of continuous membership of and regular contributions from workers. Although the trade unions are hierarchical, these hierarchies are not fixed but are based on the acceptance of democratic principles of equality and elections. In principle, anybody can occupy any post in the trade union hierarchy, irrespective of caste, creed, region or economic status.

Thus, it needs to be made clear that the working class movement is a much larger phenomenon which ***includes the trade unions***. However, it can be said that the trade unions are the most organised and modern expression of the labour movement.

DEVELOPMENT OF CAPITALIST ENTERPRISES

The working class is an integral part of the capitalist economy. Traces of capitalism were introduced in India in the 19th century under colonial dispensation. It was an ironic situation where the organisation of production was capitalistic whereas the labour market was unfree. Plantations and railways were the initial enterprises to herald the era of colonial capitalism in Indian subcontinent. A British company, the

Assam Tea Company, was established in 1839 to set up tea gardens in Assam; coffee plantations were started in South India by 1840. Companies which were organised along capitalist lines and produced for international markets established these plantations.

Port cities Bombay, Calcutta and Madras became the centres of the capitalist economy. Cotton mills in Bombay, jute mills in Calcutta, and and several factories in Madras were set up in the late 19th century. Similar developments took place in some other cities as well, i.e., Ahmedabad, Kanpur, Sholapur and Nagpur. It was mostly owned by the Indians. A Scottish entrepreneur started the first jute mill in Calcutta in 1854. It also expanded rapidly over the next fifty years. The ownership of the cotton mills was with the Indian entrepreneurs, while that of jute was of the with the foreigners for a long time. By 1914, there were 264 cotton mills in India employing 260,000 workers, 60 jute mills with 200,000 workers, the railways provided work to 600,000 people, the plantations to 700,000 workers and mines to 150,000 workers.

WORKERS' MOVEMETNS BEFORE THE EMERGENCE OF TRADE UNIONS

Even before the emergence of trade unions after the First World War there have been various forms of labour movements and protest against low wages, long working hours, inhuman conditions of work and several other issues. In fact, the trade unions can be seen as the result of these earlier labour struggles to secure their demands. The trade unions, however, were the most organised and advanced form of labour organisation when they emerged.

Although the plantations and mines contained a large number of workers who were heavily exploited. But, despite this isolation, the plantation workers, on their own, registered their protests against the exploitation and oppression by the plantation owners and managers. More active forms of protests were expressed in individual and collective violence against the assaults by the plantation authorities. All these protests were severely repressed by the planters' musclemen with the help of the colonial police. In 1884, the Bombay cotton mill workers held a big meeting and submitted their demands to the government for lesser hours of work. There were also reports of strikes among the mill workers. By the 1890s, the strikes became so frequent that the authorities spoke about a 'strike mania' among the workers. These strikes and protests increasingly began to involve more and more workers.

In other industrial centres like Calcutta, Ahmedabad, Kanpur, Madras, Nagpur and Surat the situation was almost similar. The workers were slowly learning to protest and combine for the redress of their grievances. These combinations were increasingly growing bigger involving larger number of workers. There were many people and organisations involved with these workers. In Bengal, Sasipada Banerjee initiated welfare activities among the workers since the early 1870s. He tried to educate them and to voice their grievances. For this purpose, he founded the 'Working Men's Club' in 1870 and started publishing a monthly journal in Bengali entitled Bharat Shramjibi in 1874. The Brahmo Samaj formed the 'Working Men's Mission' in Bengal in 1878 to impart moral education among the workers. It also established the 'Working Men's Institution' in 1905.

There were some organisations in this period which resembled the trade unions. The Amalgamated Society of Railway Servants of India and Burma formed in 1897, the Printers' Union in Calcutta, and the Postal Union in Bombay were among these. But they could not maintain any continuity in their functioning and were in existence for a short period only.

EMERGENCE AND GROWTH OF TRADE UNIONS Book Q.2

The Indian trade unions have developed in the specific context of colonialism and an underdeveloped economy. The problems of the developing economy still continue in the post-independence period. With lower levels of education, higher levels of unemployment and underemployment, and lower wages, the workers in India face many problems which are also reflected in the union growth.

> ### The Beginning

The trade unions emerged in India after the First World War. Further, the rising prices of essential commodities, decline in the real wages of workers, increase in the demand for the industrial products resulting in the expansion of India idustries, Gandhi's call for the non-cooperation movement, the Russian Revolution, etc., were the main factors which led to the emergence of trade unions in the post-War period in India. The Madras Labour Union, formed in April 1918, is generally considered to be the first trade union in India. B.P.Wadia, a nationalist leader and an associate of Annie Besant, was instrumental for its organisation. It was mainly an organisation based on the workers of Carnatic and Buckingham Mills in Madras. But workers from other trades such as tramways, rickshaw-pullers, etc. also joined the union in the initial stage. Around the same time, labour agitation had started in Ahmedabad which was to lead towards a completely different model of labour organisation. The workers in Ahmedabad were agitating for a bonus to compensate for the rise in prices. On the basis of this struggle and on the principle of arbitration, the Textile Labour Association, also known as Majur Mahajan, was established in Ahmedabad in 1920. This union worked along Gandhian lines and became very strong over the years. The trade union movement now picked up momentum and many more unions were formed in many centres. By 1920, according to an estimate there were 125 unions consisting of 250,000 members.

> **Formation of the AITUC and Subsequent Developments**

The All India Trade Union Congress (AITUC) was formed in 1920 as a development of these trends towards union formation all over India. Many people connected with labour realised that there was a need for a central organisation of labour to coordinate the works of the trade unions all over India. Bal Gangadhar Tilak, N.M.Joshi, B.P.Wadia, Dewan Chamanlall, Lala Lajpat Rai, Joseph Baptista and many others were trying to achieve this goal. The formation of the International Labour Organisation (ILO) in 1919 acted as a catalyst for it.

Lala Lajpat Rai became the first president of the AITUC and Joseph Baptista its vicepresitdent. Motilal Nehru and Vithalbhai Patel were also present. The AITUC received a lot of support from the Indian National Congress. It was a promising beginning and the AITUC continued to grow until it split in 1929. In the aftermath of the First World War, there were numerous strikes by the workers all over India. As expected, most of these unions were present in the advanced industrial centres like Bombay, Calcutta, Kanpur, Ahmedabad, and Madras. The main industries where these unions were formed were cotton and jute textiles, railways, shipping, iron and steel and post and telegraphs.

The Communist Party of India (**CPI**) was formed abroad in Soviet Union in October 1920. M.N.Roy was the moving force behind this. Soon after the formation of the CPI, the communists became active in the labour movements.

THE MOVEMENT IN THE POST-INDEPENDENCE PERIOD Book 3

In the post-independence period, the state became the sole arbitrator in the relationships between the industry and the working class. During this period the main concern of government was to achieve growth, industrial paece, and proper management of the conflict between workers and the management. In order to achieve these goals the state passed laws like the Industrial Dispute Act, 1947, and introduced the Labour Relations Bill and Trade Unions Bills in 1949.

The economic recession in the late 1960s caused economic hardships for the workers in the Bombay. It was reflected in the growing unemployment and financial burden of the workers. Inability of the traditional trade unions to solve problems of the working class provided a fertile ground for the birth and growth of Shiv Sena. Shiv Sena founded a trade union the Bharatiya Kamgar Sena. It emerged as an alternative to the traditional trade unions.

By the mid-1970s, there was a general feeling among different social groups the country against the organised traditional political institutions and processes like political parities and organisations affiliated to them like trade unions, elections, professional political leaders. This created resentment against such notion of politics.

In 1974 the railway workers affiliated to the main trade unions, except the Congress affiliated INTUC organised a nation-wide strike. The rail operations came to a halt during the strike. The government responded with the strong anti-worker stand and tried to break the strike.

With some exceptions the studies generally focus on the movements of the organised and formal sectors. While the political parties, especially those belonging to the left, have organised the agricultural labourers, some times the agricultural labourers have launched agitations without the leadership of trade unions on issues relating to the wages, the non-economic coercion on them, decrease in the time of working. For example, harvesters belonging to the low castes went on strike in the early 1980s in a village of western UP.

The working class movement in India is constrained by several factors. Therefore, there is no class politics in the country. In stead Indian politics is a centrist politics. Such statement overlooks the presence of a large number of trade unions and their mobilisation of the working class from time to time. No doubt, the rise of identity politics based on caste, language, religion, tribe, regions, etc., especially from the last two decades of the twentieth century pose serious challenges to unite the working class on their issues. The encouragement to the market with the decline role of the state as part of the globalisation agenda has further relegated the issues of working classes to the background.

14.2: IGNOU Book Exercise - Solved

1) What is meant by "working class movement"? Discuss the nature of the working class movement in the pre-independence period.
Answer by India Ebook: Read the 1 Shot Concept Above.

2) Write a note on emergence and growth of trade unions in India.
Answer by India Ebook: Read the 1 Shot Concept Above.

3) Discuss the main features of the working class movement in India during the post-independence period.
Answer by India Ebook: Read the 1 Shot Concept Above.

14.3: IGNOU Past 6 Attempts Question - Solved

Dec 2021: Write short notes in about 200 words each on the following:
(b) Working Class Movement in India
Answer by India Ebook: Exact same as **Q.1** above.

NOTES

____

____

____

____

____

Introduction

Socio-economic Profile

- ➤ Heterogeneity
- ➤ Dependence on Others
- ➤ Victims of Natural Disaster
- ➤ Mechanisation, Globalisation and Fisher Folks

Issues, Leadership and Organisations

Collective Actions of Fisher Folks: Some Examples

- ➤ Fisher Folks' Movement in Kerala
- ➤ Fisher Folks' Movement of Chilika Lake: Anti-Prawn Culture Agitation

15.1: One Shot Concepts

INTRODUCTION

Unlike other social groups the collective actions of the fisher folks have generally gone unnoticed in the academic discourse. This perhaps is due to the fact the collective actions by the fisher folks themselves have been relatively less in number than those of other groups. However, their problems have been raised by political parties, civil society orgnisations and church leaders. But this has been mainly in terms of demanding relief to the fisher folks who suffered due to the natural disaster like tsunami. Nevertheless, there are examples of the collective actions of the fisher folks, which can be categorised as the social movements of the fisher folks. In this unit, we will discuss their social movements.

SOCIO-ECONOMIC PROFILE   Book Q.1

➤ Heterogeneity

Fisher folks, (nearly 12 million) form a large section of the Indian population. They contribute enourmously to the economy of the country, especially the states situated along the coastlines i.e., Tamil Nadu, Kerala, Andhra Pradesh, Orissa, West Bengal, Goa, Andman Nicobar, Pondicherry, Maharashtra, Gujarat, etc. Involved in the fisheries – catching, selling, processing and marketing fish for centuries, fisher folks provide fish which form the staple of the people living in the coastal states, and also non-vegetarian population living in other states than those of the coastal regions. They also link Indian economy to the world economy through the export of the marine products. Fisher folks are not homogenous groups. They follow multiple religions, a large number of them belong to the low castes. Apart from the coastal regions, they are also found in other areas of the country involved in the fisheries, ponds and big tanks. Largely fisher folks belong to the vulnerable groups of the society.

Besides the division among them on religious and caste basis, they are stratified on the basis of ownership of vessels and employment of labour. On these basis, the fisher folks can be divided into three groups:

1) fisher folks who own vessels and work with their families;

2) Those who own these and employ other fisher folks; they include film stars, politicians and other wealthy persons.

3) Those who do not own them but work on others' vehicles.

➤ Dependence on Others

Fisher folks depend on a large number of people. The latter include intermediaries who work as the agents of traders, moneylender, non-fisher folk owners of trawlers and big boats. The fisher folks do not have direct access to the market. They sell their catch to the intermediaries (or the agents) who in tern sell them to the traders. The intermediaries take their commission and the fisher folks do not get the fair price of their catch. Their earnings are not enough to meet their basic needs which include the items of daily needs and the purchase of boats, catamarans, mechanised boats, nets, catamarans fitted with motors, etc.

➤ Victims of Natural Disaster

Their close habitat and dependence on sea for the fisheries exposes the fisher folks to natural disasters like flood, typhoon and tsunami. These natural disasters affects the fisher folks the most. They are deprived of their houses, vessels and lives. The super cyclone in Orissa in 1999 had affected the fisher folks there. The tsunami of December 26, 2004 which affected the coastal regions of South Asia and South East Asia had the devastating impact on residents and tourists of these regions. But these were the fisher folks as a single group which was affected by tsunami. It not only killed many of them and destroyed their vessels and residences, it disturbed their centuries old faith in the sea. It created fear- psychoses about the sea among the fisher folks.

➢ Mechanisation, Globalisation and Fisher Folks

Traditionally fishing was carried out by small, unpowered craft confined to shallow waters. Mechanisation began with the Indo-Norwegian Project in 1953, whereby mechanised fishing equipments were permitted to catch fish indiscriminately with the aim to increase fish catches and augment the production of shrimps. Increasing demand for shrimps from advanced countries like Japan and USA created a further impetus to intensify fishing with the use of bottom trawlers. This not only led to dwindling of fish stocks, but the traditional fishermen who were unable to afford mechanised fishing equipments began to face livelihood problems as the coastal fishing belt was captured by resourceful non-fishermen.

ISSUES, LEADERSHIP AND ORGANISATIONS

➢ Issues

The principal issues/demands on which could be collective actions of the fisher folks are organised are:

1) Participation of the fisher folks in fisheries and fishery management; sale and processing of harnessed cathes;

2) Opposition to the introduction of travelers;

3) Resource allocation and management of fisheries;

4) Providing catamarans, boats, loans/grants;

5) Rehabilitation (in case of the natural disasters) –

6) Exploitation by the agents, traders and moneylenders.

7) Others: problems arising out of bilateral relations between neighbouring countries – Sri Lanka, Bangladesh and Pakistan which include arrest of fisher folks while fishing (as they are not able to identify the demarcation of the sea line between India and these countries).

➢ Leadership   Book Q.2

Leadership to the fisher folks movements in South India is provided by the church fathers, nuns intellectual-academic activists, student-social activists, professional social workers, community organisers, social and physical scientists. Many of them belong to the fisher-folk communities. They work in league with NGOs concerned with the socioeconomic and ecological issues. Most important among them are Fr. Thomas Kocherry,

Fr. Puthhenveed. Fr. Paul Arakkal, Fr. Albert Parisavilla, Fr. Peter D'cruse. They organised the fisher-folks in Kerala on several occasions. Prof. John Kurien is known to have provided leadership to the fisher folks as an intellectual-academic activist. The leadership operates at two levels — local and national. Some of the regional levels leaders have graduated to the status of national level leaders of fisher folks.

➢ Organisations

Book Q.2

First attempts to form fisher folks' organisations at village, state and national levels in India were made in the 1960s and 1970s. The earliest union was formed in 1963 in Quilon district in Kerala. By the 1980s the unions were formed in Alleppey, Cochin, Trivendram and Malabar districts. In Kerala there was a direct linkage between the Roman Catholic church and the leadership of these organisations. But it was only in the 1980s and 1990s that these organisations mobilised fisher folks into a movement. There were fisher folks unions in other coastal states like Tamil Nadu, Gujarat, Andhra Pradesh and West Bengal. But it was in Kerala where they were most assertive and articulate. The most significant fisher folks unions in Kerala was Kerala Swatantra Malsaya Thozhilali Federation (KSMTF) or Kerala Independent Fisher Workers' Federation. In 1978 the fisher folks' unions of Goa, Tamil Nadu, Kerala and other sates formed a confederation, which came to be called as the National Fishermens Forum (NFF).

COLLECTIVE ACTIONS OF FISHER FOLKS: SOME EXAMPLES

Book Q.3

Since the 1960s there have been agitations of the fisher folks' in different forms and degrees in the coastal states of the country on some of the issues. But it was only from the 1980s that fisher folks' movement took a concrete shape. This section deals with the collective actions or the social movements of fisher folks with the help of two examples i.e., their collective actions in Kerala and Orissa.

➢ Fisher Folks' Movement in Kerala   June 2021

The first major organised movement of the fisher folks' in Kerala was in the form of protest against the introduction of trawlers, which took place in the late 1970s. During the 1970s there were several instances of the localised riots/protests of the fisher folks of Kerala. By the end of the 1970s their protest took an organised form.

The organisation which organised the fisher folks in their protest was Kerala Swatantra Malsaya Thozhilali Federation (KSMTF) or Kerala Independent Fisher Workers' Federation. Again in 1981, the KSMTF organised demonstrations in 1981 at the focal points of the 600 km. coastal lines in order to catch the attention of the policy makers and planners. The demonstration saw the participation of all age groups which included a larger number of women. The main demands of the agitators included:

1) exclusive fishing zone for the small scale fisher folks,

2) a closed season for the trawling operation "during monsoon months of June to July",

3) a total ban on the purse-seiner operations, and

4) other demands for greater welfare measures for fish workers.

The movement met with the resistance of the lobbies of the investors, intermediaries and Trawlers Boat Owners Association. One result of the movement was passage of The Kerala Marine Fisheries Regulation (KMFR) Act 1981 for regulation of harvesting zones. But the Act could not be implemented properly, though the Left and Democratic government introduced welfare measures for the benefit of the fisher folks - village societies, insurance schemes, more liberal credit, housing loans, etc. The government also appointed a committee to look into the "scientific and technological issues and assess the socio-economic consequences of the fisheries management demands of the fishermen".

The fisher folks' problems could not be solved by the legislative, administrative and political steps of the government. The KSMTF again announced launching of the monsoon movement in 1984.

The government expressed it unwillingness to ban the trawling during the monsoon period on the ground that it would result in the fall of foreign exchange and unemployment. But the NFF (National Fishermen's Forum) suggested banning of the trawling during monsoon on experimental basis; it suggested that the help of the FAO Fisheries Division be sought for providing expertise to ban trawling on experimental basis.

Towards the end of the 1980s the KSMTF took up new demands:

i) Only active fishermen should be given ownership of fishing assets,

ii) asking the government to take legal action against the trawlers/purse-seiners under the KMFR Act.

Women played very significant role in the fisher folks' movements in Kerala. In the 1990s, the fisher folks' movement achieved the national character. During the recent years Fisher folks' movement in Kerala got linked with the international movement of the fishermen in the sense that the issues raised by it were framed in the light of the report of the International Conference of Fish workers and their Supporters (ICFS) held in July 2005.

> ➢ **Fisher Folks' Movement of Chilika Lake: Anti-Prawn Culture Agitation**

Chilika Lake was a reference point of the fisher folks' movement in 1999. Chilika Lake known for the largest brackish water in Asia, is a source of livelihood to a large number of the fisher folks of Orissa. Chilika Lake was declared as wetland of international importance by the Rasar Convention. The Lake is also habitat of a large variety of biodiversity including dolphins and different migratory birds. Since 1992 an NGO, Orissa Krushak Mahasangh, with Banka Bihari Das as its president had helped to organise the local fishing communities around Chilika Lake with the with the help of the Mangrove Action Project.

Tata House sought to set up a large number of industrial scale semi-intensive shrimp farms on the shore of Chilika Lake. Tata's move was stopped mid-way as result of the court injunction. The court injunction came after the hard legal battle between the Tata House and fisher folks. The fisher folks launched an agitation against the shrimp farming in the Chilika Lake in 1999 May-July. The organisations which took lead in were Chilika Matsyajib Mahasangh, National Fisherworkers Forum NFF (India), World Forum for Fish-harvesters and Fishworkers (WFF). A large number of the fisher folks participated in the agitation. On June 11, 1999 the agitation took a violent turn resulting in police firing in which four fisher folks were killed and 13 were seriously injured.

15.2: IGNOU Book Exercise – Solved

1) Discuss the **socio-economic profile** of the fisher folks and identify their main problems.

Answer by India Ebook: Read the 1 Shot Concept Above.

2) Write a note on the leadership and organisations of the fisher folks.

Answer by India Ebook: Read the 1 Shot Concept Above.

3) How do you understand the fisher folks' movements as social movements? Explain with the help of some examples.

Answer by India Ebook: Read the 1 Shot Concept Above.

15.3: IGNOU Past 6 Attempts Question – Solved

Dec 2018: Write notes in about 200 words on each of the following: (a) Demands of Fishers Community

Answer by India Ebook: The principal **issues/demands** on which could be collective actions of the fisher folks are organised are:

1) Participation of the fisher folks in fisheries and fishery management; sale and processing of harnessed cathes;

2) Opposition to the introduction of travelers;

3) Resource allocation and management of fisheries;

4) Providing catamarans, boats, loans/grants;

5) Rehabilitation (in case of the natural disasters) –

6) Exploitation by the agents, traders and moneylenders.

7) Others: problems arising out of bilateral relations between neighbouring countries – Sri Lanka, Bangladesh and Pakistan which include arrest of fisher folks while fishing (as they are not able to identify the demarcation of the sea line between India and these countries).

Dec 2020(Feb21): Explain Fisher Folks' Movement.

Answer by India Ebook: Exact same as **Q.3** above.

June 2021: Write notes in about 200 words on each of the following: (a) Fisher folks movement in Kerala

Answer by India Ebook: Refer Concept above as Marked.

NOTES

____

____

____

16. ENVIRONMENTAL AND ECOLOGICAL MOVEMENTS

Introduction

Environmental Movements in India: Issues and Concerns

The Popular Movements

- ➢ Chipko Movement
- ➢ Appiko Movemet
- ➢ Narmada Bachao Andolan (NBA)
- ➢ Urban-based Environmental Movements

16.1: One Shot Concepts

INTRODUCTION

Environmental and ecological movements are among the important examples of the collective actions of several social groups. Protection and recognition of constitutional and democratic rights, which are not defined by law but form an important part of the day to day living of the subaltern masses like the control over their resources, the right of indigenous people to preserve their culture, protection of environment and maintenance of ecological balance are significant concerns of these movements, as they affect the human life to a great extent.

These movements also reflect an enlarged vision of economics and politics. Economic justice sought by these movements does not mean mere distribution of resources but encompass a larger vision like enhancement in the quality of life through recognition of people's right over their natural resources, their right to live with dignity, and their participation in the decision–making. The concerns of human environment received spectacular attention of scholars following the conclusion of the United Nations Conference on Human Environment, Stockholm in 1972. By the 1980s the "green movement" became a worldwide phenomenon encompassing various countries of the world including India. It is signified by several movements of people for the protection of their environmental and ecological rights in India, 'eco-greens' or 'green movement' in Germany and North Amercia.

ENVIRONMENTAL MOVEMENTS IN INDIA: ISSUES AND CONCERNS

Book Q.1

The genesis of the environmental movement in India can be traced to the Chipko movement (1973) in Garhwal region in the new state of Uttranchal. In fact, between 1970s and 1980s there were several struggles in India around issues of rights to forest and water which raised larger ecological concerns like rights of communities in forest resources, sustainability of large scale environmental projects like dams, issues of displacement and rehabilitation etc.

The Indian environmental movement is critical of the colonial model of development pursued by the post–colonial state. The post–independent state failed to build up a development agenda based on the needs of the people and continued to advocate the modern capitalist agenda which led to the destruction of environment, poverty and marginalisation of rural communities. Formation of national parks, sanctuaries, protected areas in India, in fact represents the conventional environmentalism which the Indian state advocated with the aim of preserving wildlife and biodiversity by pushing people out of these areas.

The following table is an overview of the issues, categories and examples of environmental movements, which have taken place in India:

Categories	Issues	Some Examples
Forest and land-based	• Right of access to forest resources. • Non-commercial use of natural resources. • Prevention of land degradation. • Social justice/human rights.	Chipko, Appico, tribal movements all over the country (for example, Jharkhand/Bastar Belt).
Marine resources and fisheries, aquaculature	• Ban on trawling, preventing commercialization of shrimp and pawn culture. • Protection of marine resources. • Implementation of coastal zone regulations.	National Fishermens' Forum Working for traditional fisherfolk on Kerala. Chilka Bachao Andolan, Orissa.
Industrial pollution	• Stricter pollution control measures. compensation. • Prevention of reckless expansion of industries without considering design. locational factors and livelihood issues of local population.	Zahiro Gas Morcha in Bhopal; Ganga Mukti Andolan in Bihar; movement against Harihar Polyfibre factory in Karnataka; movement against pollution of Sone river by Gwalior Rayon factory led by Vidushak Karkhana Group of Shahdol district, MP; movements against poisoning of Cheliyar river in Kerala by Kerala Shastra Sahitya Parishad (KSSP).
Development projects: a) Dams and irrigation projects	• Protection of tropical forests. • Ecological balance. • Destructive development. • Rehabilitation and resettlement of the displaced.	Silent Valley movement by KSSP; Narmada Bachao Andolan; movements against Tehri by Tehri Bandh Virodhi Samiti; the Koshi Gandhak Bodhghat and Bedthi; Bhopalpatnam and Ichampalli in the west; the Tunghbhadra, Malaprabha and Ghatprabha Schemes in the south; Koyna Project affected Committee

b) Power projects	• Ecological balance. • Rehabilitation and resettlement, high costs.	Jan Andolan in Dabhol against Enron; Koe-Karo Jan Sanghatana in Bihar. Anti-mine project in Doon valley.
c) Mining	• Depletion of natural resources.	Anti-Bauxite mine movement (Balco project) in Orissa.
d) Industrial plants/ Railway projects/ Airport project	• Land degradation. • Ecological imbalance. • Realignment. • Rehabilitation and resettlement of the displaced. • Ecological balance.	Protests and demands of Kakana Railway Realignment Action Committee. Citizen's group against Dupont Nylon 6.6. Goa. Amravati Bachao Abhyan against a large chemical complex.
e) Military bases	• Ecological balance. • Rehabilitation. • Resettlement and safety.	Anti-missiles test range in Baliapal and at Netrahat, Bihar.
Wild-life sanctuaries. National parks	• Displacement, rehabilitation and resettlement, loss of livelihood.	Ekjoot in Bhimashankar region of Maharashtra, Shramik Mukti Andolan in Sanjay Gandhi National Park, Bombay.
Tourism	• Displacement, cultural changes, social ills.	Himachal Bachao Andolan. Bailancho Saad. Goa.
Advocacy groups/ individual campaigns, citizen's Action Groups	• Policy inputs, stricter measures for protected areas. • Clear policy on national park and wild-life sanctuaries, lobbying, research, training and documentation on wild life, conservation, education, community-based environmental management. Publications on environmental issues.	Society for Clean Cities. Bombay Natural History Society (BNHS). Centre for Science and Environment (CSE), Delhi. Research, training and documentation organizations such as Bombay Environmental Action Group. Save Bombay Committee. Save Pune Citizen's Committee, etc.
Appropriate technology/ organic farming	• International debates. • Sustainable development. Eco-friendly models of development. • Low cost, environmental-friendly housing and technology.	Ralegaon Siddhi (Anna Hazare's village). SOPECOMM. Laurie Baker's Housing experiments. People's Science Institute. Dehradun.

THE POPULAR MOVEMENTS

This section discusses some of the forest-based movements, Anti-dam movements and movements caused due to the environmental pollution. The forest-based movements discussed here include Chipko and Appico movements; the anti-Dam movement includes NBA; the anti pollution–movement include those which took place in Delhi.

➤ **Chipko Movement** Book Q.2

The origin of modern environmentalism and environmental movements in India can be ascribed to the Chipko movement in the central Himalayan region in the early 1970s. Chipko movement, launched to protect the Himalayan forests from destruction, has its' roots in the pre independence days. Many struggles were organised to protest against the colonial forest policy during the early decades of 20th century. Peoples' main demand in these protests was that the benefits of the forest, especially the right to fodder, should go to local people. These struggles have continued in the post-independent era as the forest policies of independent India are no different from that of colonial ones. The origin of 'Chipko' [chipak jayenge - to hug] took place during 1973. In the early 1973 the forest department refused to allot ash trees to the Dashauli Gram Swarajya Sangha (DGSS), a local cooperative organisation based in Chamoli districts, for making agricultural implements.

Three important aspects were responsible for the success of Chipko movement. First, the close links between the livelihoods of the local people and the nature of the movement. The local people consider Chipko as a fight for basic subsistence which have been denied to them by the institutions and policies of the State (Guha, 1989). In addition, specificity of the area where Chipko movement took place; involvement of women in the contribution to households' subsistence and the overwhelming support to anti-alcohol campaign have led to the overwhelming support of women which is unique to the Chipko movement. The second aspect is with regard to the nature of agitation. Unlike other environmental movements Chipko has strictly adhered to the Gandhian tradition of freedom struggle, i.e., non–violence. Third, the simplicity and sincerity of the leaders like Sunderlal Bahuguna and their access to national leaders like Mrs. Indira Gandhi, other politicians and officials also helped to the success of the movement to a large extent.

The demands of the Chipko movement were as follows:

i) complete stoppage of cutting trees for commercial purposes;

ii) the traditional rights should be recognised on the basis of minimum needs of the people;

iii) making the arid forest green by increasing people's participation in tree cultivation;

iv) formation of village committees to manage forests;

v) development of the forest related home-based industries and making available the raw materials, money and technique for it; and

vi) giving priority to afforestation in the light of local conditions, requirements and varieties.

What is distinctive about Chipko movement is that it was the forerunner as well 'as direct inspiration for a series of popular movements in defense of community rights to natural resources. Sometimes these struggles revolved around forests, in other instances,around control and use of pasture, mineral or fish resources.

➢ Appiko Movement

Inspired by the Chipko movement the villagers of Western Ghats, in the Uttar Kannada region of Karnataka started Appiko Chalewali movement during September – November, 1983. Here the destruction of forest was caused due to commercial felling of trees for timber extraction. Natural forests of the region were felled by the contractors which resulted in soil erosion and drying up of perennial water resources. In the Saklani village in Sirsi, the forest dwellers were prevented from collecting usufructs like twigs and dried branches and non timber forest products for the purposes of fuelwood, fodder honey etc.They were denied of their customary rights to these products.

In September 1983, women and youth of the region decided to launch a movement similar to Chipko, in South India. Women and youth from Saklani and surrounding villages walked five miles to a nearby forest and hugged trees there. They forced the fellers and the contractors of the state forest department to stop cutting trees. The people demanded a ban on felling of green trees. The agitation continued for 38 days and this forced the state government to finally concede to their demands and withdrew the order for felling of trees. In October, the movement entered into its second phase and this took place in Bengaon forest Here the forest was of mix tropical semi–evergreen type and mostly on hilly terrain.

In fact Appiko movement became a symbol of people's power for their rights of natural resources vis-a-vis the state. In November, the movement spread to Nidgod village in Siddapur taluka preventing the state from commercial felling of trees in this deciduous forest of the region. The Appiko movement was successful in its three fold objectives, i.e., protection of the existing forest cover, regeneration of trees in denuded lands and utilising forest wealth with proper consideration to conservation of natural resources. Like the Chipko, the Appiko movement revived the Gandhian way of protest and mobilisation for sustainable society in which there is a balance between man and nature.

> **Narmada Bachao Andolan (NBA)**   Book Q.3

Narmada river project encompassing three major states of western India Gujarat, Madhya Pradesh and Maharashtra is the most important case study in terms of maturation of environmental movement and dynamics related to politics of development. The controversy which surrounded this project has challenged the government at all levels and at the same time was successful in creating and forging linkages with civil society organisation and NGOs, both at the national and international level.

The Narmada Valley Project, with its two mega projects- Sardar Sarovarm Project and Narmada Sagar Project in Madhya Pradesh ,is the largest single river valley project with the objective of making the world's largest man–made lake. The consequences of the project are, however, quite glaring and alarming. The reservoir will submerge 37,000 hectares of land of which 11,000 hectares are classified as forest. It will displace about one lakh persons of 248 villages- 19 of Gujarat, 36 of Maharashtra and 193 of Madhya Pradesh. The state government initiated the project as Gujarat was one of the worst water–starved regions in India and there was drastic shortage of water for domestic, commercial, agricultural and industrial needs. Further, the state had witnessed one of the worst droughts between 1985-88 which further reinforced this project.

Before the Ministry of the Environment even cleared the Narmada Valley Development Projects in 1987, the World Bank sanctioned a loan for $450 million for the largest dam, the Sardar Sarovar, in 1985. In actuality, construction on the Sardar Sarovar dam site had continued sporadically since 1961, but began in earnest in 1988. It may be mentioned here that the NBA began as a fight for information about the Narmada Valley Development Projects but developed as a fight for just rehabilitation for the lakhs of people to be ousted by the Sardar Sarovar Dam and other large dams along the Narmada river. In 1988, the NBA demanded formally the stoppage all work on the Narmada Valley Development Projects. In September 1989, more than 50,000 people gathered in the valley from all over India to pledge to fight "destructive development."

Many issues of the project are yet unresolved. However, what is more important is that the Movement has been successful a considerable extent. The achievements of the movements include:

• Exit of the World Bank from Sardar Sarovar in 1993

• Halt of Sardar Sarovar construction 1994-99

• Withdrawal of foreign investors from Maheshwar dam 1999-2001.

The NBA is unique in the sense that it underlined the importance of people's right to in formation which the authorities finally had to concede under media and popular pressure. It was successful not only in mobilising hundreds of thousands people from different walks of life to put pressure on the State government for its anti-people policies, affecting and displacing lakhs of tribals from their homes and livelihoods.

> **Urban-based Environmental Movements**   Book Q.4

In the recent past environmental pollution caused due the industrialisation has become the focus of collective action by the civil society organisations, NGOs, concerned individuals, especially lawyers, scientists, environmentalists and social activists. They sought the intervention of the judiciary and drew the attention of the state for showing concern to the pollution caused by the process of modernisation. However, the main focus of the collective action against pollution has been in the urban areas. Certain tragedies like gas leakage in Bhopal based Union Carbide MNC, Charnobyl in former Soviet Union where thousands of people were killed created worries among the people on the negative effect of the industrialisation.

Though the 1990s have seen increased concern about the environmental pollution, awareness about the disastrous impact of the environmental pollution started growing in the 1960s. All the major cities of India are facing acute air, water and other kinds on environmental pollution. Continuous immigration of the people from rural areas into the cities, their habitat in the congested areas which exist along with the polluting small scale industries; increasing number of vehicles; and unplanned expansion of cities, open drainage, etc. have created levels environmental hazards. This pollution made people susceptible to multiple diseases.

The protection of environment did not form significant part of the policies of the state. The Nehruvian model gave more emphasis to the industrialisation without showing much concern for the pollution it was going create. However, in 1976 an Constitutional Amendment called upon the state "to protect and improve the environment and to safeguard the forest and wildlife of the country" and made the fundamental duty of every citizen "to protect and improve the natural environment including forests, lakes, rivers and wildlife, and to have compassion for living creatures".

In the following decades the state passed legislations to prevent air pollution and environmental protection like The Air Act of 1981 and Environmental Protection Act of 1986. The judiciary has become the arbiter of people's rights which include their protection from the environmental protection also since the emergence of the device of the Public Interest Litigation (PIL). In the face of indifference of the executive and legislature about the people's problems, the PIL has become an effective weapon through which people seek the intervention of the state on these issues. The intervention of the judiciary forced the state to introduce some measures for prevention of environmental pollution. Justice Krishna Iyer, Justice Kuldeep Singh and advocate MC Mehta have made remarkable contribution in protection of the environment.

To sum up, environmental and ecological movements became prominent in India since the 1970s, like other such movements. The concerns of these movement are not confined to any particular groups. They are all encompassing – the entire village and urban communities, women, tribals, peasants, middle classes and nature. Even the issues raised by them concern all sections of society in varying degrees.

16.2: IGNOU Book Exercise – Solved

1) Highlight the main issues and concerns of the environmental movements in India.

Answer by India Ebook: Read the 1 Shot Concept Above.

2) Discuss the main feature of the Chipko movement.

Answer by India Ebook: Read the 1 Shot Concept Above.

3) Write a note on Narmada Bachao Andolan (NBA).

Answer by India Ebook: Read the 1 Shot Concept Above.

4) In your opinion, how are the environmental and ecological rights related to democracy and development in India? Explain.

Answer by India Ebook: Read the 1 Shot Concept Above.

16.3: IGNOU Past 6 Attempts Question – Solved

June 2021: Discuss Narmada Bachao Andolan.

Answer by India Ebook: Same as **Q.3** above.

17. SOCIAL MOVEMENTS AND DEMOCRACY: AN ASSESSMENT

Introduction
Meaning of Democracy
 ➢ Ingredients of Democracy
Limitations of Formal Democracy
Mass Politics and Mass Movements
Democracy and Social Transformation in India
Rising Expectations, Frustration and Democratic System
Movements and Democratisation
Movements Against Democracy

17.1: One Shot Concepts

INTRODUCTION

Having studied various social movements in India, we shall now examine relationship between democracy and social movements. Our purpose is to assess the role and significance of social movements in democratic political system.

Do the movements strengthen and invigorate democracy?

In other words do the movements make democracy more effective to attain its objectives?

Or do social movements hamper functioning of democracy?

MEANING OF DEMOCRACY

The word democracy is often used loosely. Political leaders of different ideologies and missions use the world democracy to suit their actions which include even imprisonment of rivals, genocide of 'other' ethnic community and violation of human rights. Recently the United State of America waged war on Iraq to establish 'democracy' there. Many dictators calim that they were working for democracy – for the welfare of the people. As a result the term creates more fire than heat or add to confusion in our understanding. Let us see some of the widely use definition:

• "Democracy comes from the Greek words demos meaning 'people' and kratos meaning 'authority' or 'power'."

• Democracy is government of the people, for the people and by the people.

• "The word 'democracy' itself means 'rule by the people'. A democracy is a system where people can change their rulers in a peaceful manner and the government is given the right to rule because the people say it may.

• "…government which is conducted with the freely given consent of the people."

• "…a system of government in which supreme authority lies with the people."

• "Rule by the people in a country directly or by representation."

In the above definitions 'people' are central in the democratic system. But people are not homogeneous. In a stratified society there are some people who are economically, socially and politically very powerful. And on the other hand, many people are powerless. They depend on the powerful for their economic survival.

> **Ingredients of Democracy**   Book Q.1

Democracy has three essential and overlapping ingredients. They are:

(1) political institutions;

(2) political processes, and

(3) substantial functioning.

In democratic system political institutions such as electoral system and legislature provide scope and necessary mechanism to citizens to participate directly or indirectly in decision making processes. They elect their representatives to from the government which takes decisions on behalf of the people for society as a whole. These representatives execute their decisions through various agencies like bureaucracy, police and military. They enjoy authority over societal resources and their management. When the citizens are not satisfied with their representatives in their functioning, decisions and use of power, people change them and elect other representatives. In that sense people have final authority who should manage the state and society. This is a formal institutional aspect of democracy.

The elected representatives cannot rule society according to their whims. Rule of law is an essential component of the democratic system. That means that the rulers/ representatives are not above law. The representatives exercise their power and take decisions within the Constitutional framework – written or by convention- that spells out their power and responsibility. In democracy political power of any one institution is not absolute. Different institutions maintain check on each other. It is a system of checks and balances.

Democracy without politics is body without soul. Politics means conflict and struggle of interests and ideologies. Politics is concerned with control over resources, their use and distribution. It involves debates and decisions on identifying priorities in policy making regarding use of resources and generation of surplus. It is a system in which different points of views and ideological formations on societal matters contest with each other. They compete for power and influence political decisions. It involves the process of monitoring political institutions and policy makers as well as the executive.

Mere elections and government of elected representative do not make the political system democratic. Democracy in substance does not mean number game: rule of, for and by majority. It cannot be called democratic system if the government by majority vote prevents dissent and opposition parties or majority wipes out minority communities or prevents them to follow their religion.

LIMITATIONS OF FORMAL DEMOCRACY

Institutions are mechanism to attain certain objectives. Their structures in terms of composition of membership, organisational system locating power and responsibilities/ duties, control over resources, procedures for functioning to take decisions and carrying out responsibilities – are formed in context of time and objectives. The institutions that may carry out functions 'successfully' at particular point of time, may not succeed at different points of time. This might be because the objectives for which the institutions were created, no longer remain important in the new situations. Or the forces outside the institutions have changed and the institutional mechanism is not able to handle them. For instance, the system of two houses in England played very important role till the mid 20th century not only to keep check on each other but also to maintain certain continuity in society and get wisdom from aristocratic and professional classes. But over a period of time the upper house becomes redundant and ornamental. Or take another example, two party system which succeeded in accommodating existing interests and providing stability in the early phase of democratic system now fails to represents all the plural and divergent interests that have emerged with further democratisation of society. No institutional structure and procedures are foolproof to meet all situations.

Institutions are important but not always enough in attaining substantial aspect of politics. They provide limited choice to the people. Social movements build pressure on policy makers for reforming institutions, create new institutions, keep check on abuse of power and demonstrate needs and expectations of people. Social movements provide avenue for social transformation, which is the objective of democracy. Moreover, as David Bayley argues that public protests have a certain 'functional utility' even in a parliamentary form of government. They keep the rulers on their toe. They also provide safety valve where people express their grievances. That gives warning to the government against rising dissatisfaction and forces; and leads to take remedial measures. Hence, social movements are complementary to democracy.

MASS POLITICS AND MASS MOVEMENTS

Some social scientists like by William Kornhauser, Robert Nisbet, Edward Shils argue that democratic system has evolved various institutions to manage societal affairs on behalf of the people. The system provides opportunities to express their desires, grievances and problems to their representatives through periodical elections. People can change their representatives in elections. But according to these scholars direct collective actions in the forms of mass movement is 'anti-democratic'. Such movements bring unnecessary pressure on the elected representatives and hamper efficient functioning of the political institutions. The government is often pulled in different directions and forced to take policy decisions under pressures rather than merits of the issues. This paves way to populist politics.

Therefore, these scholars are in favour of excluding movements from democratic system. In the 1950s and 1960s some Indian scholars who approved of the agitation for independence from foreign rule, did not approve of agitations in the post-Independence period. They condemned them outright as 'dangerous' and 'dysfunctional' for 'civilized society'. One of them argued, 'One can understand, if not justify the reasons which led the people in a dependent country to attack and destroy everything which was a symbol or an expression of foreign rule. But it is very strange that people should even now behave as if they continue to live in a dependent country ruled by foreigners'. they blame the opposition parties, leaders and trade unions for instigating the masses to direct action.

DEMOCRACY AND SOCIAL TRANSFORMATION IN INDIA

The functioning of democratic system during the last five decades has brought certain positive transformation in our traditionally hierarchical society. Brahminial framework of social order has been de-legitimised. Rule of law, equal citizenship, social and economic equality have been codified in legal system and are accepted moral principles to be maintained and attained. In the process, political positions are no longer the sole prerogative of upper castes – brahmins, rajputs and banias. Democratic system has also created various institutions that to some extent maintain checks on each other. Legal mechanism provides freedom to express opposite views and expose misdeeds of rulers. Pressures on the state are built for accountability of their actions.

After fifty years of democratic system only 40 per cent of the population enjoys basic amenities such as potable water, education and health. One fifth of the households still live in a state of 'abject', or a 'moderate' state of deprivation, such as too little drinking water, pucca (brick) house and literacy, not to speak of access to health services. In the midst of certain improvements in certain social service sectors there are also some disturbing reversals. Infant Mortality Rate (IMR) has almost stagnated in the last decade. The nutrition level and calorie intake of the poor have decline. Almost 12 million people suffer from Vitamin A deficiency.

During the last five decades of the democratic system many poor have lost their traditional resources of livelihood which used to provide them some relief to cope up with misery. Common resources like common-land, forest and water have been increasingly grabbled by the dominant classes and musclemen. In the name of so-called development the State has also take away from many tribal and non-tribal farmers their land and habitat.

RISING EXPECTATIONS, FRUSTRATION AND DEMOCRATIC SYSTEM

Number and coverage of social movements in different forms have increased in all societies including in democratic system. This is primarily because the rising aspirations of the people are not adequately met by existing political institutions which are rigid or incompetent. Many scholars such as Huntington, Rajni Kothari and several others observes that as the gap between expectations of people and performance of the system widens mass upsurge in the forms of movements increase. Alain Touraine and Jurgen Habermas argue that democratic system in post-modern society is not able to guarantee individual freedom, equality and fraternity. In the view of these theorists, democracy is degenerating into an authoritarian, technocratic state. The state in turn has become subjugated to market forces. The state's technocracy and the forces of the market thus dominate people. There are no longer workers, but only consumers. The old class of workers has ceased to be a class in production process. Instead people's main social role has become that of consumers. In this role, people are manipulated entirely by the market. For Habermas, social movements are seen as defensive reactions to defend the public and the private sphere of individuals against the inroads of the state system and market economy.

While highlighting limitations of parliamentary democracy in India **A.R. Desai** argued in 1960s:

"The parliamentary form of government, as a political institutional device, has proved to be inadequate to continue or expand concrete democratic rights of the people. This form, either operates as a shell within which the authority of capital perpetuates itself, obstructing or reducing the opportunities for people to consciously participate in the process of society, or is increasingly transforming itself into a dictatorship, where capital sheds some of its democratic pretensions and rules by open, ruthless dictatorial means. Public protests will continue till people have ended the rule of capital in those countries where it still persists. They will also continue against those bureaucratic totalitarian political regimes where the rule of capital has ended, but where due to certain peculiar historical circumstances Stalinist bureaucratic, totaliterian political regimes have emerged. The movements and protests of people will continue till adequate political institutional forms for the realization and exercise of concrete democratic rights are found."

Rajni Kothari also believes that 'democracy' in India has become a playground for growing corruption, criminalisation, repression and intimidation of large masses of the people. In such a scenario mass mobilisation at the grassroots level is both necessary and desirable. Electoral system, political parties and established trade unions do not provide space to the masses to bring social transformation. "In their place there is emerging a new arena of counteraction, of countervailing tendencies, of counter-cultural movement and more generally of a counter-challenge to existing paradigms of thought and action'.

MOVEMENTS AND DEMOCRATISATION

As we have seen above that many scholars believe that social movements play positive role in democracy in different ways.

One, social movements are the outcome of people's political consciousness. It is an expression of people's consciousness for asserting their demands.

Two, social movements encourage participation of people on political issues. While articulating agenda of the struggle the leaders discuss/ explain various aspects of the issues with the participants. Such process of discourse also contribute in developing and sharpening consciousness of the people. Political participation and consciousness of the people are backbones of democracy.

Third, success and effectiveness of social movements depend on extent of mobilisation. Greater mobilisation tends to expand political horizon and lead to further democratisation of society.

Fourth, Social movements express aspirations, needs and demands of the people who can only assert through collective action and become effective. They keep the policy makers on toe and accountable of their decisions.

Fifth, number of social movements influence policy makers and compel them to enact laws to meet their demands – advancing or protect their interests. The followings are illustrations.

During the 1920s and 1930s there were number of peasant movements in different parts of the country. Some of them were spontaneous of local peasants and some were organised by Kisan Sabha, Gandhians and left parties.

However, these laws were not implemented with speed and efficiently in most of the states. By the late 1950s series of poor peasant movements took place in different parts of the country against landlords and rich peasants. Most effective and widespread movement was Naxabari, which bean in West Bengal and spread in many parts of the country. In the 1960s socialist and Left parties organised land grab movements.

In the 1920s Dr. Ambedkar organised number of movements of dalits against untouchability which included temple entry, use of water from public tank, use of public roads etc. In 1930s he launched a movement for separate electorate. Gandhi and Hindus opposed it. Gandhi then went on fast against the demands of dalits. That lead to famous Poona Pact between Gandhi and Ambedkar.

One can assess similar kind of impact of movements such as of women, adivasis, organised working class etc. on formation of state policies on different issues. Regional and ethnic movements of Nagas and Mizos, people of Punjab, Andhra Pradesh, Gujarat, Maharashtra, Jharkhand, Uttarakhand etc. resulted into formation of linguistic or ethnic states.

MOVEMENTS AGAINST DEMOCRACY

However, it should be emphasised that all social movements per se do not necessarily lead to more democratisation. History has witnessed in India and elsewhere that some social movements oppose social transformation. They may be called counter-movements. People are mobilised to resist change coming from the oppressed sections of society. Anti-reservation agitation in 1980s is a case in point. The upper caste students were against the reservation for the Scheduled castes, Scheduled Tribes and Other backward castes. They launched agitation and succeeded to some extent in preventing the government for the implementation of reservation policy for the OBCs. The movement for Ramjanma Bhumi and Hindu Rastra is another example.

17.2: IGNOU Book Exercise – Solved

1) Discuss the main components of democracy and explain why is politics central in democracy?

Answer by India Ebook: Read the 1 Shot Concept Above.

2) Analyse working of democratic system in India. According to you does it meet the expectations of majority of the people? Why do you say so?

Answer by India Ebook: Refer Concept.

3) Why are social movements important in democratic system?

Answer by India Ebook: Read Concept Above.

4) Do all social movements enhance democratic process? If not why?

Answer by India Ebook: Read the 1 Shot Concept Above.

17.3: IGNOU Past 6 Attempts Question – Solved

Dec 2018: Discuss how state can accommodate social movements in democratising and decision-making.

June 2020: Discuss the relevance of social movements in Indian democracy.

Dec 2021: Discuss social transformation under present Indian democracy.

Ans: Do it Yourself from the above Concept.